Also from Brassey's

MAKEPEACE-WARNE
Brassey's Companion to the British Army

ZADKA
Blood in Zion:
How the Jewish Guerrillas drove the British out of Palestine

DAVID
Mutiny at Salerno: An Injustice Exposed

BREAKING RANKS

Social Change in Military Communities

Christopher Jessup

Brassey's
London • Washington

First English Edition 1996

UK editorial offices: Brassey's Ltd, 33 John Street,
London WC1N 2AT
UK orders: Marston Book Services, PO Box 269,
Abingdon, OX14 4SD

North American orders: Brassey's Inc, PO Box 960,
Herndon, VA 22070

Christopher Jessup has asserted his moral right to be
identified as the author of this work.

Library of Congress Cataloging in Publication Data
available

British Library Cataloguing in Publication Data
A catalogue record for this book is available from the
British Library

ISBN 1 85753 045 4 Hardcover

Typeset by M Rules
Printed in Great Britain by BPC Wheatons, Exeter

For Di, with love
and gratitude

Contents

Foreword

In 1987 Ruth Jolly concluded her examination of the inter-relationship between careers in the armed forces and the family lives of military employees with an explicit plea for change:-

> The military has much to offer, but it has always been a conservative institution, resistant to change and especially to social change. Pointless lamentations over supposedly 'declining standards' and futile attempts to 'restore' them will not help the situation one bit. The Services should work out new policies to adapt to today's circumstances. If they insist on standing, Canute-like, on the shore trying to turn back the tide of social change, they may find themselves suddenly in deep water, floundering.
>
> (*Military Man, Family Man: Crown Property?*, Ruth Jolly; London: Brassey's, 1987)

This book advances the discussion to take account of subsequent social, economic and military developments, and speculates on the changes in management style which military institutions will be forced to adopt by the end of the century. Its focus is not on the operational and logistical aspects of Service life, but on how such activities impact on military employees and their families. In particular, the changing characteristics both of Service personnel and especially of their families are examined in detail.

The book grew out of a professional educational involvement over many years in training people employed to further the welfare of Service families. This connection destroyed many of the stereotypes about military life which, like the majority of civilians, I had formerly believed. It enabled me to observe from close quarters how major institutional systems sought to accommodate themselves to fierce winds of change, and to develop a respect for organisations which strove to retain a system of values whose concern with valour, honour and meritorious conduct clung determinedly to a philosophy which stressed the superiority of communal and collective concerns over personal gain.

Military organisations have historically functioned as total institutions, able to dictate not only the working life of their employees but to a large extent to control private and family life as well. Such power, however paternalistically or benevolently used, has come to be seen as archaic and intolerable to the current generation of Service families. How those institutions might adapt to such changing perceptions amongst their own populations is the subject of this book. Failure to evolve will prejudice not only recruitment but also the retention of expensively trained personnel. Ignoring or denying social change has enormous cost and operational implications for the armed forces, for whom the 'ostrich position' is not a credible long-term choice.

Although mainly concerned with the United Kingdom, comparisons have been drawn with American experience and practice to provide a wider frame of reference.

Acknowledgements

Many people – consciously or otherwise – have helped shape this book. In particular, Services personnel attending 'Support for Service Families' welfare training courses in Bristol, Germany and Hong Kong have provided valuable insights into the social dimensions of military lives. Physically visiting and meeting families in their married quarters has been especially fruitful in enabling me to inhabit, if only briefly, other peoples' reality. Lieutenant Colonel (retired) John Sims, formerly Principal Housing & Welfare Commandant for British Forces Hong Kong, and his counterparts in G1 Division, HQ British Army of the Rhine (now United Kingdom Support Command Germany) were instrumental in providing me with such opportunities. Knowledge and experience have been generously made available to me over many years by the Controllers of the British Army Families Housing and Welfare Service, Lieutenant Colonel (retired) Tony Lerwill and his successor Brigadier (retired) Bill Winder. Captain David Lockyer RN, former Chief Staff Officer of the Naval and Personal Family Service, and Nick Bennett, Area Community Officer at Plymouth within the NPFS, arranged useful occasions when I was able to meet with substantial numbers of Royal Navy welfare personnel. Contributing evidence to The Army Wives

Study and to the 1993 Tri-Service Enquiry into Welfare brought me into productive contact with Colonel Mike Gaffney and Brigadier Adrian Naughten. I am especially grateful to Lieutenant Colonel David S Wolpert, Head of the Family Policy and Research Unit of the United States Air Force, who responded most helpfully to a request for information about USAF welfare services and related matters.

These individuals, and many others, have offered me their time and expertise. They are, of course, in no way responsible for the uses to which I have put the material in this book, and would probably disagree with some of my conclusions.

At Brassey's, I should like to thank General Tony Trythall, Jenny Shaw and Caroline Bolton for their hospitality and encouragement at a time when the company was itself negotiating as turbulent a period in its history as many of the military families described in this book.

In preparing the manuscript, I am deeply indebted to Sandra Powell of the Department for Continuing Education at Bristol University, whose pre-eminent word-processing skills were able to compensate more than adequately for my own deficiencies.

Above all I must thank my partner and colleague Diana Brothers, Director of the Diploma in Counselling courses at Bristol University. In a very real sense, she was the inspiration for this study and contributed invaluably to an earlier draft.

I am grateful too to copyright holders for permission to quote from the following works:

Dartmouth Publishing Company for the use of data from the *British Social Attitudes Surveys* 1984 and 1989.

The Ministry of Defence for permission to quote parts of the *Discipline and Standards Paper* (Ref. D/AG/1993) and the *Continuous Attitudes Surveys: Officers (Report 93RO27); Soldiers (Report 93RO37);* and *Wives (Report 94RO23).*

Introduction

It was 0230 hours on a Monday morning when the Families Welfare Officer was woken by a phone call from the guardroom. A soldier had barricaded himself and his wife and two very young children in their third floor flat. He appeared to be very drunk and was dangling his four-week old baby daughter over the edge of the balcony threatening to drop her. He had his wife in a stranglehold with his other arm. He was demanding, very loudly, to see a General to sort out a grievance about early discharge from the Army.

This was the dramatic emergency confronting a British Army unit in Cyprus recently. The guardroom, alerted by disturbed neighbours unable to sleep, immediately contacted the Families Officer, grateful to be able to delegate a difficult domestic incident.

The Families Officer – an Army Captain, promoted from the ranks after 18 years' service and tasked with promoting the well-being of Army families – had several options. One would have been to comply with the drunken demand and bring a General to listen to the soldier's complaint. This line of action failed to commend itself to the Families Officer on two grounds. Firstly because no General was actually present in the garrison area at the time; and secondly because the

Families Officer doubted strongly that his own career would be advanced by inviting any General who could be located to demonstrate the quality of his decision-making by assuming command at 0300.

The more practical alternative adopted was to arrange for the local fire service to position jump blankets immediately beneath the balcony and for the Families Officer to commence negotiation through the locked apartment door with the soldier. Eventually, returning sobriety together with assurances that his grievances would be investigated persuaded the 23-year-old infantryman to release his family, unlock the door and be marched into temporary detention.

Such sensational events are fortunately rare, but less dramatic requests for help and support in managing to combine private lives with military careers present themselves frequently to the welfare systems of contemporary armed forces. Lying behind this particular problem was a marital history of continual separation, erratic duty hours and unanticipated geographical moves. The soldier's wife – a professionally-qualified nurse – had been unable to continue in her employment in Cyprus, and had also lost out in terms of status and superiority because of previous moves. She had become highly critical of the impact of the Army on her life and had sought with increasing vehemence to persuade her husband to leave. Despite the substantial redundancy programme which followed the end of the Cold War, the Army had refused to accept the soldier's application for discharge. Trapped between intolerable domestic pressures and what appeared to him to be inexplicable obstinacy from the Army, the soldier achieved widespread publicity for his case through his self-imposed siege. However, he did not in fact manage to leave the Army until two years later.

What this story neatly illustrates is the complex interrelationship of domestic and working lives. This book examines such interaction in the context of British and American armed forces where families are required to manage particularly turbulent and demanding lifestyles. Achieving and sustaining adult personal relationships and family goals *and* simultaneously maintaining the highest degree of professional military competence – including the capability to deploy anywhere with little advance warning – demands a highly skilled balancing act. It is hardly surprising that not all military households manage this at all times.

Although the pressures applied to armed forces families are more extreme than those confronting most civilians, there are growing similarities. Increasing social and occupational mobility is a common feature of both the British and American social fabric, and for the UK these trends will accelerate as a consequence of a closer British involvement within the European Union. Just as for Service Personnel, employment patterns will take on an added spatial dimension for many civilians.

Moreover there are other social trends inducing enormous changes in the traditional relationships between military families and the parent Service. Foremost amongst these are the changing expectations of married partners about the structure of their own relationship and the degree of time and privacy they can legitimately expect. Higher educational standards and a greater awareness of what quality of life is possible have undermined the social structure founded on benevolent paternalism which has characterised the relationship between military institutions and families in the past. Role expectations within marriage – especially the movement towards greater domestic equality – fit uneasily into the demands of military life.

Similarly, the career expectations of spouses have assumed as equal an importance in armed forces families as amongst civilians. Lifestyles, and life quality, depend critically on sustaining two incomes. Yet achieving and maintaining dual-career status is particularly difficult for Services households exposed to geographical turbulence every 18 months and erratic marital separations which make planning the career paths of partners extremely problematic.

The outline of this study is as follows: Chapter One reviews the social forces that are compelling change within contemporary families and the conflict between these developing expectations and the social structures of traditional British and American military communities; Chapter Two discusses the problems of courtship and partner-choice for armed forces personnel and the incentive towards early marriage provided by the patterns of the early stages of a military career; Chapter Three explores the consequential pressures on military marriages and child production; and Chapter Four examines divorce in military communities. Chapters Five to Seven look at social changes threatening traditional military institutions. *The Rise and Rise of the Professional Woman* examines the implications of gender equality for the military workforce. *Farewell to Loyal Campfollowers?* reveals the growing revolt amongst spouses to participation in those social systems and lifestyles approved of and supported by military mores. And in *Sex: the DS Solution*, the increasing challenge from the gay community to the patterns of heterosexual orthodoxy sanctioned by the military establishment is charted.

In conclusion, Chapters Eight and Nine examine *The Metamorphosis of Military Communities*. What pro-active approaches are available to military institutions enabling successful adaptation to major change? What communal and social structures match both the expectations and needs of Service families and the operational specifications of command? Does the repatriation of British and American personnel from overseas bases spell the end of military cantonments segregated from civilian environments? Or will Service personnel increasingly occupy housing in civilian areas and become virtually indistinguishable from other occupational groups? Can much vaunted social systems designed to promote unit integration – 'regimental tradition' – survive such geographical dispersion? Hitherto, employment within the armed forces has normally involved relative isolation from civilian environments. Re-entry into civilian communities demands major attitudinal change, and is often experienced as an unwelcome culture shock. However, the ending of the Cold War and the subsequent withdrawal of British and American forces from overseas bases implies less exclusivity attached to military careers in future. Moreover, recent events have torpedoed the comforting belief in the security of employment offered by the armed forces which has long been seen as an important factor compensating for some of the less desirable features of Service life. But if the

military can no longer guarantee job security, what degree of
employee loyalty can still be reasonably anticipated?

All the cases used in this book are true. They are problems
which have happened to real people. However, the names, locations and other identifying details have been changed to prevent
identification.

CHAPTER 1

Disaffection in the Ranks?

Yet the modern world . . . continues to spawn organizations and groups which . . . make total claims on their members and which attempt to encompass within their circle the whole personality. These might be called *greedy institutions* insofar as they seek exclusive and undivided loyalty . . . Their demands on the person are omnivorous. . . . Greedy institutions are characterised by the fact that they exercise pressure on component individuals to weaken their ties, or not form any ties, with other institutions or persons that might make claims that conflict with their own demands.

(*Greedy Institutions: Patterns of Undivided Commitment,*
Lewis Coser; New York: The Free Press, 1974)

Military employers have always sought total commitment from their employees, and the right to require instant professional readiness at all times. Such obligations are typified by the continuing practice of the British armed forces in publishing salary rates on the basis of a 24-hour day. Each day receives specified remuneration, *but each day is wholly available to the employer.* Although in practice leave is routinely built into the expected annual employment pattern of all Services personnel, it does not figure in the daily pledge of total availability which forms the essence of a contractual relationship enabling the employer to legitimise unlimited demands.

The armed forces clearly epitomise Coser's concept of the greedy institution. This has been made possible historically by their exemption from the forces of social control which have interceded on the part of employees in establishing tolerable working conditions and contracts. Trade union activities have been specifically outlawed by legislation from British and American Services. As a result, the military employer has been enabled to impose the demand of an unlimited commitment on all Services personnel, a demand which has major implications for families. Indeed, only within the past 30 years have military institutions acknowledged the existence of families and begun to provide support systems assisting them to manage within the uncertain world of military employment. Such support has not, however, been unconditional. In return, family members have been expected to follow lifestyles and patterns of behaviour approved by the military employer. Such expectations have often been experienced as interference and intrusion by family members – especially spouses who are conscious that they have no contractual commitment with the Service but are nevertheless bound by loyalty to their serving partners to participate in activities prescribed and approved by the military employer or risk the possibility of adverse career repercussions for the military employee.

GREEDY FAMILIES IN A TOTAL ENVIRONMENT

However, families have themselves been characterised as greedy institutions as well. Mady Wechsler Segal analysing 'The Military and the Family as Greedy Institutions' in *Armed Forces and Society* (Vol. 13, No. 1: Fall 1986) concluded that:

> While it [the military employer] exerts some specific normative pressures directly on family members, most pressures affecting families are exerted indirectly through claims made on the Service members. For both types of pressure, the family is expected to adapt to the greediness of the military institution and support the Service member in meeting military obligations. However, important

societal trends in general and in military family patterns in particular are making this adaptability problematic. Because of these trends, which include changes in women's roles in society (especially labor force participation rates), as well as increases in the numbers of married junior enlisted personnel, sole parents, active duty mothers, and dual-Service couples, military families themselves are becoming greedier, increasing the potential conflict between the military and the family.

Living in a military community is analogous to living in a 'company town'. One sole employer provides subsidised housing, frequently medical, educational, community and social welfare facilities, and often institutionally-approved supermarkets exclusively serving military families and offering attractive tax concessions on alcohol and tobacco products. Where British and American armed forces have been located overseas, such communities have been established in preference to attempting any integration with the host nation, and undoubtedly the establishment of familiar British or American social and commercial practices rather than utilising foreign provision has been welcomed by the families concerned.

However, the military has dictated the price for transporting native customs and facilities where bases have been located: total loyalty from the employees. Thus, the military has been able effectively to control the *total environment* within which both employees and family members are sustained. Such communal isolation has been justified on grounds of potential military threat and the need therefore for logistical autonomy. But such social structures have also proved extremely convenient to senior military managers, since through them subtle pressures could be exerted on employees to guarantee conformist behaviour.

BREAKING OUT

Challenges to the benevolent (but autocratic) paternalism of the 'company town' have emerged from Services personnel themselves, but in the main, and more prominently, from spouses and other family dependants who have perceived the enforced lifestyle as manipulative, sexist and patriarchal. As the majority of military employees marry at some point during their contract, spouses have become far more numerous, and military communities typically now comprise a majority of married personnel. Generated by these changes in demography has been the emergence of spouse support groups: the Federation of Army Wives and The Association of RAF Wives in the UK has paralleled the development of the Military Families Association in America. These organisations have become sufficiently important to be consulted by military hierarchies automatically on issues perceived as impacting on families – especially housing quality matters. However, these Associations have sought more active roles than merely being consulted. They have successfully taken the initiative in seeking, and achieving, changes in those military practices found to be particularly objectionable. In the UK, for example, military planners must now include in deployment calculations information about the schooling stages of dependent children before deciding on postings for the Service employee who is also a parent, since geographical moves frequently dictate that schools have to be changed.

In both British and American armed forces, marriages tend to occur at younger ages than for civilians. The reasons for this are examined in the next Chapter, but it is important to acknowledge at this point that not only have military communities become predominantly married societies, they have become *young* married societies too. The unique requirements of engaging in military employment thus affect an increasing number of marriages, many of them negotiating the first critical five years of matrimony. Although married:unmarried ratios rise with age and rank, the proportion of even the most junior ranks married has grown markedly for both countries since 1970. One outcome of this has been the decreasing availability of junior NCOs to share leisure-time activities with their platoon members – a tendency much regretted by senior officers who perceive here the origins of section leaders 'failing to get to know their men' [sic] – a process which was allegedly managed far more successfully in the past. But married junior NCOs have to maintain a delicate balance between the voracity of two greedy institutions, anxious to satisfy both family expectations and professional endeavours. Crucially, they will have moved into family housing and will no longer share accommodation with other unit personnel, and it is this physical separation which hampers the institution's goal of leisure-time interaction between leaders and led.

THE DEMANDS OF A MILITARY LIFE

Military institutions make four major demands on employees and their families. Firstly, by its very nature, the profession of arms carries with it an above-average risk of injury or death. Of course, it can be assumed that as Service personnel have chosen this particular career for themselves, some degree of personal equanimity in the face of the potential personal risks must have been achieved or the individuals concerned would not have enlisted in the first place. However, even if this were true initially, marriage induces a different perspective on personal danger for the more mature Service person, and, in any case, members of military families are never likely to share the same degree of composure towards the threats intrinsic in military occupations.

Secondly, military families are exposed to many more frequent geographical movements than civilians. Described as 'turbulence' within the British armed forces, such relocations occur on average every 16 months within the British Army (see *Report of The Army Welfare Inquiry Committee*, Ministry of Defence, 1975 and *The Army Wives Study*, M and J Gaffney; Ministry of Defence, 1986). High rates of mobility are experienced in the US Services too, where both officers and enlisted ranks can anticipate moving at least once every three years. (*Description of Officers and Enlisted Personnel in the US Armed Forces: Reference for Military Manpower Analysis*, Z D Doering and W P Hutzler, RAND, 1982).

Whilst some military families welcome geographical variety, moving house remains a high stress inducer. Moreover, it becomes less and less attractive as family members become older and experience greater losses by leaving a known environment.

5

Frequently, too, the move may occur without the family receiving much notice. 'Average' deployment lengths disguise the fact that for some households moving twice within 12 months can be a fairly typical experience. Certainly within the British armed forces, anybody contracting for a career period of 22 years could realistically expect to move on 12 occasions. At least one Army officer, with a career of 32 years ending in 1988, moved 37 times in the 28 years in which he was married.

Thirdly, Service employees are far more likely than their civilian counterparts to be separated from their families because of professional commitments. These may take the form of training exercises, residential updating and promotion courses or unaccompanied postings. Sailors have traditionally always needed to adjust to this last form of separation, since seatime service has never been accompanied. But in the other Services too, separation from spouse and children is a regular feature of military life. Between 50–75% of British Army personnel will spend some time separated from their families during any 12-month period, a ratio very similar to US Department of Defense statistics which indicate that 55% of enlisted personnel and 63% of officers experience family separation over a similar timespan.

Separations may amount to no more than a few days, but, in the case of seatime or unaccompanied deployments such as Northern Ireland or Bosnia, the period is normally four–six months. Whatever the frequency and length, separations impose particular stresses on marriage and family relationships and figure quite high in the list of factors determining re-engagement decisions. Unaccompanied deployment because of international or domestic peacekeeping roles is more easily tolerated by family members – if they are old enough to understand what is happening – than separation resulting from unexpected training or educational requirements, even though these may be relatively short. The constant interruption of marital, parental and domestic roles which separation causes poses severe threats to all military marriages and is a source of deep resentment to many spouses (see Chapter 3 for a wider discussion of the strategies adopted within military families to manage periods of separation).

Fourthly, military personnel and their families are far more likely to be deployed overseas than most civilians. Indeed the geographical and logistical dictates of the Cold War required the permanent location of US and British land and air forces in Germany. Many operational units had no *raison d'être* outside that environment, and never moved from Germany. Although unit personnel *did* change, relocation might be to another foreign posting rather than back to the UK or the continental United States. When the Berlin Wall was destroyed in 1989, it was not unusual to find British Army personnel who had served for 10–12 years continuously in Germany, albeit at different locations. Accompanied by their families and often enjoying better quality housing than they had experienced in the UK, such families had often adjusted to living outside Britain – and indeed positively preferred to do so.

However, the attractions of foreign postings depend crucially on the precise location, the age of family members, the availability of employment for spouses and the reactions of the host community. The lack of spouse employment has confronted US and British Service families posted overseas as a perennial problem, and, despite the existence of schools funded from the Ministry of Defence budget, foreign postings have resulted in painful educational choices for British Army and RAF families in particular. Should the local, competent military schools be used for their children, or should residential schools back in the UK be preferred instead? Often UK boarding schools have been chosen in order to achieve curriculum stability, but with considerable financial implications for the family.

FAMILY CHANGE

The pressures imposed on Service personnel and their families by military employers are not new. In some respects they are less onerous than those endured by former members of the armed forces – for example, separation periods within naval service are now shorter. Nevertheless the professional demands made by the military on its staff are substantially different from those inflicted by most civilian employers. Moreover they are being borne by military communities with substantially higher proportions married than in previous comparable historical periods, and those marriages are also contending with the sweeping consequences of changes in family structure and functioning.

Foremost amongst these developments is the increase in the percentage of married women in paid employment. This has been particularly marked in Britain:

Married Women in the UK:
Economically Active

1951	21.7%
1971	42.2%
1991	70.0%

(Source: *Social Trends*, No. 9 (1979)
and No. 23 (1993)

Although approximately 50% of married women work only part-time in Britain, the virtual doubling of women in employment in the labour market in the 20-year period following 1971 has inevitably affected family organisation.

Families are greedy for the scarce resources of their adult members – especially time – yet the changing pattern of employment has clearly reduced the energy, attention and other capacities which can be directed inwards to family concerns. It is no coincidence that these changes in female participation rates in the labour force have been accompanied by lamentations about the collapse of families. Both in America and Britain, *family policy* achieved a high political profile in the 1990s with concern that social security and welfare systems exerted perverse pressures which encouraged sole parenthood, and that expansion in the proportion of married women working implied lessened, and sometimes inadequate, care and attention to children – a serious neglect for which society later paid a high price in terms of maladaptive or illegal social behaviour as the children became teenagers.

In Britain, social unease about contemporary family developments and their long-term outcomes achieved political prominence in the 'Back to Basics' campaign of the Conservative government during 1993–94. Although this collapsed in some ignominy as the result of revelations about the personal lives of several government Ministers, the sentiments expressed by Michael Howard, Home Secretary, in October 1993 undoubtedly represented widespread public support not confined simply to his own party:

> We must emphasise our belief that the traditional two-parent family is best. Best for the parents, best for society and above all best for the children.

Evidence from a major longitudinal study following the lives of all children born in one week in May 1958 was produced by Kathleen Kiernan for the *Family Policy Studies Centre* in 1991. This demonstrated that a series of presumed undesirable behaviour patterns – leaving school at the earliest possible age; leaving home by 18 years old; leaving home because of family friction; and cohabiting by the age of 20 – were more common amongst children living with a lone mother than in two-parent families. Risk rates were even higher where remarriage had occurred and the child was living with a step-parent. This induced a report from the Royal Society of Arts in March 1994 – *Start Right* – which was principally about the virtues of expanding pre-school education, but which proposed that prospective parents should enter into contracts to stay together until their youngest child reached adulthood.

Such a proposal is impracticable, and unfortunately research studies on the impact of divorce on children also show clearly that living in the atmosphere of poisonous anger which often precedes marriage breakdown is equally damaging. Having parents who have become unhappy with each other, whether they divorce or not, is undeniably bad for children. Even if all parents know this to be true, such knowledge will not unfortunately provide a guarantee of mutual happiness. Indeed, such social analysis is simplistic. Families operating in the real world – especially in the transformed realm of economic reality – have had to modify their own internal structures to accommodate social change. In particular, some degree of role transfer between adult family members has occurred, and the expectations of marital partners have clearly moved towards greater equality in both employment and domestic roles. These issues are discussed further in Chapter 2.

Military families have not been immune to changing family and employment patterns. However, spouse employment has always been more problematic within military communities, and the proportion of wives married to Servicemen benefiting from paid employment has consistently been lower than amongst civilians. This has been particularly true for military families based overseas where spouse work opportunities have generally been limited in number and menial in character. Where spouses do work, pressures on their Service partners to adopt a higher profile in domestic and child management roles have inevitably become a source of conflict with the employer's objective of total commitment – clearly impossible where time and other personal resources are being diverted to family functioning.

Resentment from both spouses and military employees at the claims made by the Services has been enhanced by the recognition that some practices hostile to the continued well-being of families – notably separation – have actually increased since the demise of the Soviet Union. International peacekeeping commitments have inflicted additional unaccompanied deployments on military strengths which have simultaneously been subjected to severe manpower and equipment reductions in search of peace dividends. 'Overstretch' is the term used by the British Armed Forces to describe a situation in which an undiminished number of liabilities dictated by the political climate are undertaken by attenuated resources.

More generally, such situations are recognised as producing personal stress. Military employers have been able to exploit the depressed economic conditions of Western Europe since 1990, retaining staff who might otherwise have sought alternative and less pressured employment. Retention of skilled personnel will, however, become much more difficult if economic recovery generates a wider range of employment opportunities. Spouses are clearly influential in instigating early retirement decisions (described as *Pre Voluntary Release* in the British armed forces), and such pressure will grow if improved civilian employment conditions coincide with the continuing impact of overstretch on family objectives such as the move towards greater role equality.

DEMOGRAPHIC DEVELOPMENTS AND THE MILITARY

Threats to the stranglehold enjoyed by military institutions over their members emerged not only from modifications in the internal dynamics of families, but also from unfavourable trends in population composition. Declining birth rates since 1970 have diminished the age range within the population from which the armed forces have traditionally recruited, as the following table illustrates:

Changes in Population of 16–19 year olds: United Kingdom (millions)

1987	1995	% Change 1987–1995
2.92	2.21	– 24%

(Source: *OPCS Population Trends*)

The situation is in some respects worse for the armed forces than these nationwide average figures suggest. Historically, in the United Kingdom, recruitment to the Services has come disproportionately from Scotland and the northern half of England, but these areas are experiencing an above-average decline in the numbers of young people aged 16–19. The drop in numbers is 28% in Manchester, 31% in South Yorkshire, and 32% in Merseyside, for example, all of which are historically important areas for engaging future military employees. These population trends obviously represent a serious threat to all employers needing to recruit from this particular age range. Foremost amongst such employers are the Services. However, what was perceived as a demographic time-bomb by many in the armed forces has turned out to date to be something of a damp squib and the predicted difficulties of obtaining Service entrants have so far failed to materialise.

The reasons for this have been fortuitous: the end of the Cold War coinciding with severe economic depression in Britain and some other western European nations. Any revival in these economies which brought with it heightened demands for young people to enter the labour force would, however, raise again the spectre of a restricted recruitment base and undoubtedly increase hiring costs for the Services. Even after the substantial personnel reductions they have sustained since 1989, the British and American armed forces remain extremely large employers. In Britain the turnover rate of people leaving the Services is approximately 12% – some 30,000 annually. The great majority have to be replaced, but obtaining staff with the appropriate educational credentials and the relevant skills-mix has become more costly. And having found, hired and often trained suitable personnel, military employers have to contend with poaching from rivals, principally in the defence equipment provision industries, who are also confronting identical skill shortages.

RETAINING TRAINED PERSONNEL

Despite the existence of high unemployment rates in recent years, on both sides of the Atlantic staff retention has emerged as *the* key issue in human resources management. In private industry and in public sector services, employers have widened their traditional personnel functions to protect the expensive investments made in hiring and training staff. Human resource management has been identified as needing a range of counselling and other support services often categorised as Employee Assistance or Occupational Welfare Programmes.

Typically, in addition to providing, or financing, personal counselling services, these employee support programmes offer advice on issues such as the management of personal finances, post-trauma debriefing for staff exposed to unpleasant experiences, and produce action strategies designed to diminish stress for individual staff members. Crucially, employee welfare agencies legitimise the disclosure by individuals of marital and domestic problems to a confidential service which overtly acknowledges the interaction between the personal and the professional life of employees and responds with a range of helping strategies, a process operating in the interests both of employer and staff. Concern about retention and re-engagement rates has led all the armed forces of Britain and the United States to develop Service-specific occupational welfare agencies. These vary considerably within as well as between the two countries in their scope and funding. The most extensive provision currently is made by the US Air Force through its Family Support Centers (FSC) which have the following overall objectives:

> Changes in social values, family structures and lifestyles require increased focus on programs and policies that foster a positive family environment. It is Air Force policy that commanders are responsible for the health and welfare of Air Force families. To assist commanders to meet this responsibility, FSC are established on active duty installations.
>
> The mission of the FSC is to support Air Force readiness and retention by helping families adapt to the demands of Air Force life and assist the commanders in response to family concerns. The FSC is chartered as a primary prevention agency and functions to ensure resources required to support families are available.
>
> (*Family Support Centre Program* AF Regulation 30–7; USAF 1991)

FSC Regulations outline staffing requirements to achieve these objectives and commit USAF Headquarters to produce resources which allow the FSC Program to function effectively. Such programs guarantee USAF families a wide range of support services, which include:

An Information, Referral Counselling and Follow-up Service
This is described as . . . 'the key function of the FSC mission' and is designed to enable families . . . 'to identify and clarify problems and needs in order to determine appropriate forms of assistance and resources. Follow-up is accomplished to ensure appropriate referral and adequate services are being received.'
Education and Skills Development
FSCs offer education and skills development assistance to enable families to adapt more readily to the stresses of military life.

Employment Resource Program
This section of the FSC enhances the employability of Air Force personnel *and their spouses.*

Transition Assistance Program
The TAP offers retiring USAF members *and their families* skills and knowledge relevant to making a successful transition into civilian life.

Personal Financial Management Program
'The Air Force offers financial information, education and personal financial counselling to enable Air Force personnel *and their families* to maintain financial stability and meet financial goals.'

In Britain, the Royal Navy provides the most comprehensive occupational welfare system to its members. The RAF offers the least developed support package, with the Army occupying an intermediate position. None of them ensures such overt recognition of the needs and rights of family members to the degree identified within the US Air Force.

The Naval and Personal Family Service (NPFS), established in the Royal Navy in April 1977 after exhaustive reviews of welfare needs, exists to offer support irrespective of rank to all members of the Navy and their families. The two principal objectives of the organisation are:

to offer to all Naval personnel and their families advice, assistance or practical help if and when needed;

to assist the Commanding Officer and his representatives in dealing with their responsibilities for the well-being of Naval personnel and their families, whether Officer or Rating, man or woman, single or married.

To achieve these objectives, the NPFS has three constituent bodies:

The Naval Family Service
Consisting of qualified social workers and support staff, this section of the NPFS provides a confidential service to Naval staff and their families who require assistance in dealing with personal problems.

The Naval Community Service

Community Officers are in post in areas where the largest concentrations of Naval families occur. Their aim is to encourage community activities in areas where Naval families live, and to maintain good community relations with the wider locality. Physical resources in the shape of community centres have been made available to provide focal points for Naval communities.

Sailors and Families Advice Bureaux (SAFAB)

Located in the main UK base-port areas, SAFABs provide a Naval equivalent to the civilian Citizens Advice Bureau. Staffed by Naval personnel with CAB training, SAFABs offer confidential and accessible information on a wide range of subjects from house-purchase to local bus timetables. SAFABs can also provide access to a money advice service for individuals needing help with personal financial planning. Like their civilian counterparts, SAFABs do not dispense personal counselling services, but can refer clients with such needs to the Family Service section of the NPFS.

Such systems have emerged, of course, because in both countries the military have been faced with the twin problems of a hostile demographic recruiting environment, and the threat of expensively trained personnel resigning to avoid further damage to family or domestic life.

In the UK armed forces, employee welfare agencies have grown with difficulty since 1974 (the foundation year of the precursor body to the *Naval and Personal Family Service*). Internal opponents have challenged the validity of channelling defence expenditure to 'welfare', and old hands – 'the old and bold' – bemoan the inadequacies of contemporary Service personnel whose need for such support indicates only too regrettably that times have changed for the worse.

In both countries, it is above all the need to retain trained personnel which has justified the expansion of occupational welfare within the armed forces. Family support systems are designed to reduce the disadvantages of military life not in a spirit of Defence Department benevolence but specifically to avoid expensive human assets becoming dispirited, and sufficiently disenchanted to resign.

Summary

The demands made by the armed forces on their employees are all-embracing, exacting heavy contributions from military families. The ability of Service personnel to negotiate favourable contractual and employment conditions is weakened by legally-enforced prohibitions on trade union membership. Consequently, military employers have enjoyed considerable freedom in determining working conditions and in imposing high commitment requirements.

However, the significant increase in the proportion of Service personnel who are married – constituting the majority in most military communities – together with increased labour force participation from women has brought to the forefront the additional demands of the military institution's major competitor: the family. Contemporary dual-career nuclear families make heavy demands on adult resources, notably time. Unsurprisingly, organisations have emerged to represent these modern families to press their case within military communities and to require that families and family members achieve recognition as individuals with rights and status.

In addition to the demographic changes resulting from more and earlier marriages within military societies, birth rate changes have seriously reduced the traditional labour pool from which the armed forces have predominantly recruited. This remains a potential future problem for organisations with high annual turnover rates of labour, although it is masked in the short term by the cessation of the Cold War and economic decline, especially in the UK. The costs of engaging appropriate new personnel has already risen in the 1990s, and a key managerial objective consequently has been identified as the retention of existing, expensively-trained staff. To this end, all the armed forces of Britain and the United States have developed various forms of occupational welfare agencies designed to encourage retention by developing increasingly pro-active support programmes intended to succour and sustain families coping with the stresses of military life.

CHAPTER 2

Partner Choice and Courtship Patterns in Military Life

Marriage as a social arrangement creates for the individual the sort of order in which he can experience his life as making sense.

('Marriage and the Construction of Reality'; P Berger and H Kellner in *Recent Sociology* (ed) H P Dreizel; New York, 1970)

. . . did she love her husband? He suddenly appeared a stranger who she hardly knew. Three months earlier she had not been aware of his existence; now she was his wife. What did it all mean? Why should one fall into marriage so quickly, as into an abyss suddenly yawning before one's feet?

(*A Woman's Life*; Guy de Maupassant; 1883)

PRESSURE TO MARRY

Young adults are expected in our society to replace the emotional support initially provided by families with a substitute based on personal choice and normally derived from their peer group. Out of the peer group emerges an individual of particular significance, and it is this person who becomes the partner for the young adult and becomes invested with the highest expectations as the source of emotional sustenance.

The pressures to marry and establish couple-partnerships are intense in Britain and America. Over 90% of British adults marry at least once. Despite the feminist critique of marriage as an arrangement designed by men to assure their creature comforts and the continuing subordination of women, the marriage intentions of currently unmarried young women seem likely to ensure the enduring popularity of marriage.

Concern that the opportunity to form a partnership is passing us by can also provide a pressure to enter a couple relationship. For Jane Austen's heroines, 23 was apparently the critical age: beyond that beckoned permanent spinsterdom if no partner had appeared by then. Honoré de Balzac raised the period for possible romance somewhat – to the age of 30. Today there is no age this side of death which is regarded as exempt from love, but there are strong family and social expectations that partnerships, normally heterosexual, will have been formed by the mid-twenties. Most young adults are strongly influenced by these pressures, although frequently the relationship formed will be expressed through cohabitation rather than a legally constituted and officially recorded marriage.

COHABITATION TRENDS

The scale on which a period of cohabitation either precedes or replaces legal marriage in northern Europe and North America is truly remarkable: a veritable social revolution, though seldom acknowledged as such. And the extent and speed with which this has occurred is phenomenal. For example, in Britain only 1% of women marrying before age 25 in the period 1960–1964 had lived with their husbands before marriage. By 1992 14% of brides under 25 lived with their partners before marriage; and 30% of brides in the age group 25–34 did so. Couples where at least one of them was marrying for the second time are more likely than not to precede legal marriage with a period of living together. As Colin Gibson points out:

> We are witnessing important demographic and social changes in long-held habits, and it is as yet uncertain where they will lead to. What is clear is that couples are increasingly living together in stable relationships and raising children out of wedlock.
>
> (*Dissolving Wedlock*; Colin Gibson; Routledge; 1994, p. 115)

This sweeping trend towards cohabitation preceding or replacing marriage is less common in military communities. Particularly for members of the British Services, cohabitation has frequently not been a practical option, partly because it was financially more rewarding to occupy military housing than to compete on the open market, partly too because actual or alleged security concerns dictated that Service personnel be grouped collectively together rather than dispersed within civilian communities. As a result moving off-base and into privately arranged accommodation – with or without a cohabitee – was effectively discouraged.

CHOOSING PARTNERS

Young Service personnel reflect prevailing pro-couple social attitudes. However, there are a number of features about their lifestyles which obstruct the patterns of courtship and partner-choice followed by civilians. There are also elements of military life which positively incite precipitate marriage choices – the desire to escape from communal life in barrack or training-block, for example; the tempting availability of Service-provided cheap housing, for which the main occupancy condition is a marriage certificate; and institutional barriers to cohabitation.

Partner choice – along with employment preference – constitutes a major demonstration of adult status. But how that partner becomes chosen depends on a combination of events and circumstances – in effect, on chance – as well as on the application of both conscious and unconscious selection procedures.

Military relationships have to surmount considerable difficulties during the courtship period. The discontinuities caused by mobility and initial training requirements impose considerable barriers to establishing stable pre-marriage partnerships. This is clearly illustrated by examining the circumstances facing new entrants to the British armed forces:

• Service recruits come disproportionately from the north of England or Scotland but their initial employment training is

invariably in areas distant from their homes, and therefore distant too from peer group acquaintances, including girlfriends;
* most recruits come from urban areas but are located during training, and often afterwards, in the countryside; and
* post-initial training and deployment is equally likely to be distant from the area of origin, and in the case of the Army in particular, may well be overseas.

Induction and initial training periods in the armed forces deliberately seek the total immersion of recruits into their new lifestyle in order to produce rapid minimum competence levels, along with uninterrupted exposure to pro-military values. Such a swift socialisation process may enable a speedy transition from civilian to Service life, but it does so at the price of reducing the links between trainees and their previous environment – including not only their families of origin but potential partners as well. Military employment expands the range of possible marriage partners – because of the variety of geographical settings in which young personnel are located – but at the same time interferes with the development of any in-depth relationship by limiting the frequency of face-to-face contact and shared experience. As a result, courtship lengths for Service marriages are often quite short.

Brief courtships – and by this is meant periods of 12 months or less – allow insufficient time for couples to undertake crucial explorations of each other. Courtships need to be sufficiently long to permit two key developmental tasks to be achieved:

* the opportunity to explore facets of each other's personality, which is what the term 'getting to know somebody' necessarily implies; and
* the chance to rehearse how a life together might work out, primarily by exchanging and comparing ideas about 'who should do what' in a marriage: making vital comparisons about rules, roles and their demarcation.

In *The Beginning of the Rest of Your Life: a Portrait of Newly Wed Marriage* Penny Mansfield and Jean Collard (London:

Macmillan, 1988) emphasise the significance of courtship as a period for exploring self-identity and consciously seeking to control the future by making a significant life choice: a marriage partner. Their newly-wed sample had generally begun exploratory searches for partners from their mid-teen years, and the majority had experienced a number of transitory friendships and at least one more serious relationship with somebody other than their eventual marriage partner.

The choice of partner which an individual eventually makes is the culmination of a lengthy process of sifting and sorting. The motives for that choice are strongly influenced, consciously or otherwise, by what Alfred Schutz has categorised as *because* choices and *in order to* choices. (*The Concept of Action: Collected Papers of Alfred Schutz*; 1962). *Because* choices relate to the past experience of an individual: they reflect a behavourist view of human action which characterises choice as largely illusory, the inevitable product of previous events. *In order to* choices express the motivation to bring about a preferred state of affairs in the future. These choices imply free-will and a belief on the part of the chooser that personal choice is meaningful and offers a strategy for controlling future prospects.

Courtship provides an opportunity for an individual to reflect on the grounds for making a particular partnership choice. Acknowledging personal motives and recognising those of a possible partner demands complex perceptions and responses. Because marriage involves a major transition to a new life-stage, analysing its nature and desired outcome requires both time and regular personal contact with the selected partner. Brief time-spans, or being physically separated obviously hinder these processes.

COURTSHIP PATTERNS

Employment and training patterns which complicate or prevent couples learning about each other increase the natural risks to which all relationships are prey. Courtships of less than a year approximately double the chances of divorce before the fifteenth wedding anniversary, yet in many military marriages the time-periods available to enable acquaintanceships to develop depth and explore compatibility are significantly shorter. Training and employment patterns which produce discontinuities in personal relationships generate difficulties in maintaining contacts with potential partners, and this leads to two identifiable consequences:

- employees suffer such pressure from a potential, but distant, partner, that performance at work deteriorates; or
- alternatively, attempts at maintaining systematic contact with former peer group members are abandoned, so increasing the probability that the eventual marriage partner will be chosen on the basis of only a short association.

Young Service recruits may seek to maintain close contact with a potential partner from whom they are now separated by employment requirements. Though this is inherently desirable, there are times when such an attempt produces problems affecting work performance, as the following Royal Air Force example demonstrates:

James Longley is 18 and one year into his post-initial training course, which has another six months to run. He copes well with the academic requirements of his course, but is currently facing a disciplinary charge for unlicensed absence – taking weekend leave without due authorisation. Interviewed by his immediate superior, Longley offered the following explanation.

His girlfriend (Sue) lives in Hull, about 180 miles away from Longley's present location. She has become very insistent that he should spend more time with her, culminating in a recent letter which was the immediate cause of Longley's absence last weekend. Sue had written:

'Jim
Come on man, when are you going to see me again? All this crap about the RAF keeping you in at weekends – you're not a little boy any more now . . . or are you?
Guess who's turned up anyway from our old crowd: Mike

22

Dempster. He's on leave from the merchant navy and has a *fantastic* tan. He seems really keen on me, and has asked me out three times this week. Don't worry – I still prefer you – when you're here. So how about a trip here this weekend to show you still really care?

> love, Sue'

Longley has known Sue for about two years off and on. She is the only 'serious' girlfriend he has ever had, and he felt that if he did not appear at Hull last weekend, he would certainly lose her.

What this case demonstrates are the pressures experienced by a competent young recruit who is anxious both to acquire new professional skills quickly, but prepared to challenge the social control systems of this new world when confronted with such a powerful personal threat: the loss of the only significant other-sex peer relationship. Such conflicting pressures dictate the need for sensitive pastoral care to protect the Service's investment in recruiting and training new personnel. Responses to rule infractions which operate only in a disciplinary mode are unlikely to achieve this.

THE LURE OF MARRIED QUARTERS

Deeper relationships are not facilitated either by the accommodation pattern experienced by Service recruits and junior personnel. Barrack-block or other styles of shared, institutional housing are the norm. Such communal living in dormitories or shared flatlets severely limits the privacy available to single people, and the desire for more personal space outside the jurisdiction of the Service undoubtedly becomes a powerful impetus towards marriage.

Although such a desire can be met by renting or purchasing private property, institutional constraints within the British armed forces to single personnel living off-base were only relaxed towards the end of the 1980s. In part, such limitations reflected security concerns that Service personnel living within civilian communities offered easy targets to terrorists. More powerful, however, was the desire of senior military staff to preserve a social situation in which unmarried junior NCOs would share their off-duty periods with basic grade recruits, and continue their inculcation into the approved Service way of life.

This method of social control theoretically ensured harmony and conformity, but if it worked at all, it did so at the cost of robbing personnel already moving up the career ladder of personal space and time. Moreover, new recruits were often equally unenthusiastic at being forced to share more than the parade ground and the classroom with NCOs who happened to be unmarried. For both groups, therefore, there were equally strong pressures for an exodus from communal accommodation, and if living off-base was either prohibitively expensive or prevented by the dictates of commanding officers, the solution was to marry.

Within the British armed forces, subsidised housing has been provided for all married personnel since 1970. The ostensible justification for this was the belief that Ministry of Defence provision was more cost-effective than individual negotiations for housing in the private market, and the practical difficulty that in many of the areas where the Services wished to concentrate in large numbers, little housing existed. Married quarters were seen as particularly supportive to young newly married couples whose financial circumstances severely limited their access to any other appropriate housing. In practice, military housing constituted tied accommodation and offered an extra dimension of control over Service personnel: misdemeanours which warranted dismissal would also lead to homelessness.

Once the minimum age limits on married quarters occupation – 25 for an officer, 21 for other ranks – were removed in 1970, military housing estates developed a very youthful profile. Married teenagers became quite common inhabitants, frequently marrying after brief courtships and to satisfy a variety of personal needs which might be neither fully understood by the partners nor mutually compatible. But a compelling force was often the need to *escape* present circumstances. For the Service person, this was often the cumulative effect of enforced communal living.

Significantly, the Army Personnel Research Establishment's *Continuous Attitude Survey* for soldiers for the period ending September 1993 highlights clearly that single personnel are consistently less satisfied than married soldiers with their accommodation. The Report comments: 'Satisfaction with accommodation remains constantly at a low level.' (APRE *Continuous Attitude Survey (Soldiers)*; September 1993) For their potential marriage partner, unattractive features in civilian life – unemployment or unreliable employment, or conflict with parents or other kin over crowded housing space – together with the desire to achieve the status of being married, could be equally persuasive in identifying marriage as the solution to life's problems. Service personnel who could offer fully furnished housing as part of an individual dowry were thus particularly attractive. The existence of married quarters was an encouragement to legal marriage – since they could not be allocated to cohabitees – and enabled youthful couples to marry earlier than would have been the case in civilian life.

Age at first marriage – for both bride and groom – rose steadily in the UK in the last quarter of the twentieth century, largely as the result of a growing trend for a period of cohabitation to precede marriage.

Average Age at First Marriage

	1971	1992
Brides	23.0	26.0
Grooms	24.8	27.7

(Source: *Social Trends*, No. 25, 1995)

As a corollary of these trends, marriage rates involving very young couples fell.

Young Marriages: Age at Marriage in 1992 (England and Wales)

	Total	Aged Under 20	%
Bridegrooms	311,564	3,883	1.2%
Brides	311,564	15,018	4.8%

(Source: OPCS *Marriage and Divorce Statistics*, 1992)

The small proportions of people marrying under the age of 20 shown in the Table above continues a trend evident in the United Kingdom since the early 1970s.

Proportion of Males/Females Aged 16–19 who are Married

	1973	1988
Males	11%	2%
Females	32%	8%

However, military communities do not parallel these civilian trends. There seems little doubt that easier access to housing, coupled with the other pressures to abandon the limited attractions of the single life, result even in the mid-1990s in a much higher proportion of Service marriages in which either the bride or groom, or both, are less than 20 years old. A visit to any married quarters estate brings home forcefully and very visibly just how young are many of the couples seeking to make a success of marriage in a military society.

OVERSEAS DEPLOYMENTS AND
INTERNATIONAL MARRIAGES

Another scenario which is commonly observed in the armed services is the hastily negotiated marriage which precedes a foreign posting. The haste is sometimes dictated by pregnancy, but more often the underlying motive appears to be a recognition that a substantial overseas tour is about to happen and that permanent other-sex company during the next two years in

Germany or Northern Ireland is highly desirable but also problematic. Because of this uncertainty about the supply of potential partners in these overseas locations, it therefore makes sense to enter into a relationship before departure, and to do so in the way legally sanctioned by the military system – official marriage. Particularly in the British Army, the weeks leading to a new overseas posting see a flurry in marital activity. No known research has been undertaken on the stability and duration of these marriages, but anecdotal evidence from Army welfare sources suggest that such partnerships experience above average breakdown rates.

The corollary to the marriage contracted in haste before an overseas deployment is the marriage between personnel stationed overseas and a native partner. In practice, it is young Servicemen rather than Servicewomen who marry foreigners, and since for British armed forces personnel the option of cohabitation has been even less available overseas than in the UK, the prevailing circumstances in effect force the couple into a legal marriage in order that they can get to know each other. Linguistic and cultural differences can become highly damaging to such international marriages when they are translated to mainland Britain or the United States, and foreign wives of UK or American Servicemen are especially prone to problems of loneliness and isolation after leaving their homeland.

Statistically, such relationships have an above average degree of risk, in the sense that they are more likely to end in divorce or separation than partnerships formed by a UK or continental United States couple. Cultural practices and expectations, religious, language and family differences can all combine to torpedo such marriages, which are also sometimes based on the briefest of courtships. Marital violence is also statistically more likely when the couple are of different nationalities – a further indicator that such relationships are exposed to high levels of conflict.

COMPATIBLE EXPECTATIONS OF MARRIAGE?

What expectations do young Service personnel have of marriage? There is no reason to suppose that they are inherently different from those held by the civilian population, nor that their motives for entering marriage vary either.

In Britain the vast majority of marriages, whether legal or informal, are founded on individual choice. Although parents in particular, and some other relatives and peers will exert some influence, ultimately personal decisions prevail, and can legally do so irrespective of parental or other opposition. This contrasts with arranged marriages where families determine the field of eligibles, and may even specify the particular partner. Individual choice is the hallmark of contemporary Western relationships, and would appear to be based on the following:

• Love; escape; pregnancy; financial security; a regular and safe sexual relationship; the demonstration of adult status by living with a partner; the desire for companionship; the desire for children and access to independent housing

Although in Western societies 'love' will usually be proffered as the dominant motive for establishing a relationship, it is by no means the only reason, as the list above illustrates. For most people there will be a mixture of pressures to marry, and this may remain for some time unrecognised. But eventually, these needs surface and the relationship has to be capable of satisfying them. Sometimes the underlying needs – to demonstrate the arrival at full adult status, for example, by living with a partner *who is expected to behave in particular ways*, or the desire for a child – may have a disconcerting impact on the relationship, overwhelming sentiments of love and affection and bewildering the couple concerned.

The presumptions which most people form about what a marriage relationship will be like derive from two primary sources. Firstly, from our family of origin. For most people this provides their most important model of what marriage is like. Our attitudes to the roles that have to be carried out in a marriage, how to resolve conflict when it occurs – on these vital matters it is the families into which we are born which significantly mould us.

Secondly, however, we are also continuously exposed to

media portrayals of marriage and family life. The happy corn-flake family – two adults, one of each sex, with their clean, shining son and daughter crunching contentedly together – is a potent symbol. The reality of breakfast in family histories prob-ably rarely corresponded to this sanitised media model, and yet from such images we derive the expectation that breakfast times (and, by extension, the whole of marriage and family life) real-ly can and *should* be like this. If the young couple in a new relationship discover their own situation to be markedly less appealing than the televised and desired image of marital life, will they succeed in recognising that this is because the media deals in fantasies, while they inhabit reality? Or will they instead search for deficiencies within the relationship, including in par-ticular the attitudes and behaviour of the partner? It is a key task for young adult partners to turn 'love' into the more per-manent condition of a loving relationship. Achieving that necessitates discarding some of the myths with which our cul-ture has surrounded marriage, and recognising that managing the real world is both harder and more rewarding.

Training and deployment patterns in the armed forces may provoke conflict over expected domestic gender roles. Not only are there severe limitations on military partners pursuing their own careers (see Chapter 6) but the periodic, and some-times unpredictable, absences from home of Service personnel prevent an equality of sharing in domestic management roles which unmarried people claim they are expressly seeking from marriage.

What mutual interaction do young couples expect of each other? Periodically, this is examined in the series of reports enti-tled *The British Social Attitudes Surveys*. There was a particular focus on the expectations and experiences of people aged 18–24 – both married and unmarried – in the 1984 Survey (see p. 30).

Social Attitude surveys have shown those aged 18–24 to be consistently more egalitarian than the general population as a whole. The determining variable, however, appears to be mar-ital status rather than youth *per se*. The young unmarried – especially unmarried women – were considerably more egali-tarian towards household tasks than were young married

	Preparation of evening meal	Household cleaning	Household shopping	Washing and ironing
All unmarried 18–24 task *should* be shared equally	51%	60%	68%	31%
Unmarried women 18–24 task *should* be shared equally	60%	61%	79%	40%
Total Married task *is* shared equally	17%	24%	44%	10%
Married 18–24 task *is* shared equally	21%	24%	56%	22%

(Source: *British Social Attitudes*, R Jowell and C Airey (eds);
Aldershot: Gower; 1984)

couples in their performance of them. Such marked discrepancies between pre-marital expectations and post-marital reality provide fruitful areas of conflict and suggest that the movement towards symmetricality in marriage has not occurred as fast as was confidently predicted in an influential work on British family life in 1973:

> By the next century society will have moved from (a) one demanding job for the wife (i.e. in the home) and one for the husband (i.e. in paid work) through (b) two demanding jobs for the wife and one for the husband, to (c) two demanding jobs for the wife and two for the husband. The symmetry will be complete. Instead of two jobs, there will be four.
>
> (*The Symmetrical Family*, M Young and P Willmott;
> London: Routledge.)

There is, however, evidence of some – albeit extremely slow – movement towards role symmetricality. *British Attitude Surveys* in 1984, 1987 and 1989 examined expectations and practice in relation to a number of domestic roles.

Asking the question 'Who is the person mainly responsible for domestic duties?' produced the following numbers saying that an itemised list of domestic tasks were equally shared:

1984	12.2%
1987	13.1%
1989	13.7%

This certainly suggests that evolution rather than revolution is at work here. Nevertheless, in answer to the prescriptive question 'Who should undertake domestic duties?' clear trends emerge in the proportion responding that the following tasks 'should be shared equally':

	1984	**1987**
Shopping	63%	68%
Cleaning	48%	54%
Care of sick children	47%	51%

In practice, the roles – both domestic and outside the home – played by marital partners may well deviate from desired and expected equality for a host of reasons, many of them outside the immediate control of the couple concerned. Research also indicates that newly-weds are in practice less egalitarian than their pre-married selves: a pattern quickly emerges in Britain of husbands as primary breadwinners, and wives as secondary earners with major domestic responsibilities. Couples typically justify this arrangement by reference to anticipated parenthood – a life-stage marked by clear divisions in domestic labour. ('Fathers in Dual-Earner Households' by J Brannen and P Moss in *Reassessing Fatherhood*, C Lewis and M O'Brien (eds); London: Sage Publications, 1987)

Military lifestyles do not facilitate the move towards egalitarianism. Specifically, the periods of separation to which young couples are exposed often make inoperable planned role demarcation. Moreover, such absences also frustrate the development of a more *companionate* marriage which is perhaps a more fundamental expectation which contemporary young couples bring into their marriages.

> Psychological intimacy between husband and wife, an intermingling of their social worlds, and a more equitable distribution of power in marriage are undoubtedly areas in which marriage in general has changed. But the importance of women's enduring role as housewives and as the main rearers of children continues.

These conclusions from Ann Oakley in *The Sociology of Housework* (Oxford: Blackwell, 1974) remain valid. But the desire expressed by wives for greater intimacy and accord with their husbands presupposes the capacity and willingness of men to respond, and certainly the ability of military husbands to meet such enhanced emotional targets is inhibited by their engagement in the Services. Role disjunction may therefore be little worse for military couples than for civilians. Achieving physical and emotional companionship, on the other hand, is threatened more severely.

PRE-MARITAL EDUCATION

In our society, people normally select their own partners. Sometimes they will move into relationships for what seem to observers the 'wrong' reasons: for instance, to escape from their current situations. That some people will see marriage as a means of deliverance from intolerable conditions is hardly surprising. However, in one sense 'escapist' marriages start with a considerable advantage: at least one of the parties has left behind something to which there is no wish to return.

Many employers may feel their young employees would benefit from exposure to a pre-marital education package. But can or should employers actually try to undertake such a process themselves? The British Army has made a number of interesting pioneering attempts at doing this, although it has to be said that the Army's pre-marital education programme has not so far had any obvious impact on the ages at which soldiers marry or the lengths of pre-marital courtships.

In 1981 the Army's Chaplain General's Department sponsored

a short video entitled *For Better, for Worse*, which portrayed a series of disasters afflicting a young, escapist marriage in which a teenage bride finally resorts to an overdose in a despairing cry for help as she confronts a permanently screaming premature baby and a young, immature and usually absent husband. The intention was to show the film to all young unmarried Army personnel. The message of the film was stark: do not marry young, and plan the timing of children carefully.

However, shock/horror tactics have limited value as a preventive strategy if the audience can successfully avoid identifying with the characters. The audience research that has been conducted on this film does suggest that the prevalent response amongst those as yet unmarried is 'that will never happen to me'. Interestingly enough, the viewing audience which does identify with both the characters and the situations portrayed generally consists of young married couples. For them the video affords an invaluable aid on which to base discussion on the management of marriage problems in an Army setting. But, in one sense, this is too late – they are already married.

As a supplement to the film some family welfare officers in the Army initiated pre-marriage information guidelines. Customarily, these usually took the form of brief leaflets offering information considered relevant by the authors. Distributed to single Service personnel, the objective was to offer information about military lifestyles to their potential marriage partners. What follows is a typical example of the genre:

Discussion Points for Soldiers Considering Marriage
General
The aim of these notes is to make soldiers who are contemplating marriage aware of the problems which frequently arise in Service marriages. It is strongly advised that these points be discussed with fiancees, parents and prospective parents-in-law before marriage, so that you and your wife-to-be move into married quarters without any doubts about the problems and difficulties which you will certainly have to face.

For those young readers insufficiently discouraged by these comments from proceeding with their rash intentions of marriage, further dire warnings follow:

Married Quarters
Many soldiers seem to think that a married quarter will be available to them on the day of marriage. This is not the case. There is usually a waiting list and it may be several weeks after the marriage before a married quarter is allocated and until then it is your responsibility to provide accommodation for your wife.

Parents
Have you discussed fully your marriage with both sets of parents? Are they in favour of the marriage? Can you count on their support when needed, for example during an illness or when your wife has a baby?

Finance
You must appreciate that when you are married, your pay will have to support two people. If you 'drink with the lads' most nights, this will have to be drastically reduced – otherwise you will certainly be unable to manage financially and will cause friction between you and your wife. Fuel and light bills are a constant problem. These are bills which must be paid, and it is therefore strongly advised that you open Budget Accounts with the Electricity/Gas authorities to spread the financial burden evenly over the year.

Beware of easy credit! Too many soldiers and their families decide to buy a video, stereo, fridge, washing machine, car etc. on credit all at the same time and then discover they owe more money than they earn. Instead, your financial management should take account of the need to save a small amount regularly. If you don't, you will never have a holiday, and when babies come along, you will not be prepared for the expenses they incur.

And, finally, the crunching put-down to marriage for those still unwise enough to name the day . . .

Separation

Don't forget that soldiering comes first and inevitably you will be away a good deal on training exercises. Does your wife-to-be know this? Could she manage on her own in a flat in Germany without you?

Not all the pre-marital education messages devised by family welfare officers are as blunt or off-putting as this. Many provide useful information with humour, but do seek also to convey the idea that setting up as a couple has many implications which need thinking through. Getting these leaflets to potential partners is, of course, highly problematic. The Army has no knowledge of who they are, where they are, or even if they exist. The first occasion on which the military system becomes aware of a forthcoming marriage is when a young soldier turns up with his bride and seeks a married quarter. Although in theory soldiers about to marry are required to inform the Army of this intention, in practice many do not, and it is not an enforceable rule. Distributing pre-marital material to fiancées or any other potential partner can really only be achieved through the man himself, and therefore with his compliance. Hence anti-marriage messages are unlikely to be delivered if the serviceman bothers to read the content and realises that it might not reinforce his romance. As with the film, there is no evidence that information leaflets of this kind have altered British Army marriage patterns in any way at all.

What has, however, been achieved is to raise awareness within line management of the close relationship between marriage and employment performance: what is personal and private directly affects what is public and professional.

Summary

Armed forces personnel are exposed to exactly the same pressures to marry as their civilian peers. Yet the opportunities to engage in cohabitation rather than legal marriage remain more limited. The practical barriers to marriage are reduced in military communities by the provision of subsidised housing, and the very existence of such housing offers an escape route to single

Service personnel seeking enlarged personal space and increased privacy. Married people are widely perceived as enjoying a superior quality of life. A simple solution presents itself: get married.

Not only do military practices invite early marriage, they also pose threats to contemporary expectations held by the partners as to what marriage should be like. The very patterns of military recruitment, training and initial deployments conflict with expectations of mutuality and sharing in domestic and work roles. Frequent geographical movement and physical separation are not easy cornerstones on which to base new marriages, and they are likely to thwart expectations of 'sharing'.

Pre-marital educational material distributed by the employer does not appear to have achieved any dramatic reduction in the number of young British Army marriages.

CHAPTER 3

Managing Military Marriages

Now, if you must marry, take care she is old –
A troop-sergeant's widow is nicest, I'm told,
For beauty won't help if your rations is cold,
Nor love ain't enough for a soldier.
(from *The Young British Soldier*
by Rudyard Kipling)

Marriage performs many functions, including providing the opportunity for unmarried people to demonstrate to society as a whole their achievement of maturity and adult status. Marriage also enables people to consolidate and shape their own lives. As Berger and Kellner have pointed out:

Marriage as a social arrangement . . . creates for the individual the sort of order in which he can experience his life as making sense.
(P Berger and H Kellner in *Recent Sociology No. 2: Patterns of Communicative Behaviour*, H P Dreitzel (ed); New York: Macmillan, 1970)

According to these authors, the individual turns to the private world of home and marriage conscious of his own authority and power to shape and control these dimensions of his life, in contrast to the turbulent and uncontrollable forces which dictate the worlds of employment and public institutions. Getting married involves two individuals coming together, redefining themselves, and sharing common future horizons. This sense of shared objectives provides also a comforting reassurance of mutual control and stability in what is otherwise perceived as a highly uncertain world.

The proportion of military personnel who marry whilst serving has grown steadily in both Britain and America in recent years. In 1992 the US Department of Defense conducted a very large-scale survey (the total sample was 96,830) of officers, enlisted ranks and spouses. Amongst other information, this study produced the following marital status data:

Marital Status of Military Personnel

Currently married	62.3%
Never been married	28.8%
Divorced or separated	8.7%
Widowed	0.2%

Of the Currently Married Personnel

Married for the first time	77.5%
Married for second or later time	22.5%

A higher proportion of American Services stationed in the US are married than those based overseas, and the American Air Force and Army contain more married people than the Navy or the Marine Corps. The median age for those who are both married and parents is the 26–34 age range. 7.6% are in joint Service marriages. The British armed forces display comparable marriage rates, with overall rates ranging from 55–65% between the three Services.

The exposition of marriage described by Berger and Kellner focused on a number of crucial perspectives which have been the basis of later marital studies, in particular the British study of partner choice and young marriage *The Beginning of the Rest of Your Life* by Penny Mansfield and Jean Collard (London: Macmillan, 1988). These were:

• the process of transition involved in becoming married;
• the dynamics of establishing interactive relationships; and
• the assumptions the couple hold about the future.

As has been already shown, unmarried people reveal a wide range of motives for marrying, not all of them conscious ones. Expectations about marriage are shaped predominantly by families of origin, social observation and media images of contemporary marriage, and the spectrum of motives and expectations will be similar in any particular society for all individuals – whether they are civilians or attached to military institutions. Military personnel and their spouses and family members will therefore share the prevailing attitudes towards marriage and family life that are dominant in their own cultures. In order to remain in being, all marriages have to negotiate and overcome challenges, and military marriages are no different in this respect from those contracted by civilians. Nevertheless, there are significant differences between the range of life events which will be encompassed within a typical military marriage and those experienced by civilian couples. In the discussion which follows, features which are peculiar to military lifestyles will be described as *Endogenous Factors*, and issues affecting marriages not unique to the armed forces as *Exogenous Factors*.

ENDOGENOUS FACTORS IN MILITARY MARRIAGES

Military marriages are exposed to a variety of circumstances which impose stresses over and above those inevitably occurring in any marriage relationship. Some civilians, of course, do also experience to a degree some of these circumstances too, but it is the combination of events and the frequency with which these episodes occur which pose exceptional challenges to couples in military marriages. There are six major endogenous factors:

• issues arising out of accommodation;
• issues arising from turbulence/geographic mobility;

- concerns about the education of children;
- limitations on spouse employment opportunities;
- the management of temporary separations; and
- issues arising from accompanied overseas deployments.

Accommodation

Military institutions in Britain and the USA provide housing for married personnel. The extent to which they do this varies somewhat between the two countries, and between the Services of either country. For example, the British Royal Navy specifically encourages its members to acquire their own homes – and, indeed, offers financial support in the form of a long-term interest-free loan – to enable them to achieve this. As a result, approximately two-thirds of Navy families are owner-occupiers, a proportion very similar to the civilian population.

In contrast, the British Army and Royal Air Force have pursued policies of 'accompanied service' – that is to say, that spouses and families should, wherever possible, live with the military employee. To facilitate this, military housing is provided at or near duty stations, and no encouragement to home ownership has been offered. As a consequence of these policies, the UK armed forces have become providers of property and related services on a very large scale, owning some 69,000 accommodation units – mostly houses – in 1995.

For the consumers of military housing, four key issues arise. Firstly, the availability of accommodation at any particular location reflects previous housing provision in that area. Not every incoming family can always expect immediate access to Service housing, and having to wait for suitable accommodation to become available involves separation, since the Service employee will be found a billet at the new workstation rather than have the commencement of work delayed until family housing is feasible.

Secondly, decisions have to be made as to the extent to which families themselves furnish military houses. Standard – and standardised – furniture is available in all British married quarters, but families increasingly elect to replace Service items with their own personal choices in order to stamp their own individuality on their military surroundings. Dispensing with military furniture produces marginal rent reductions in the charges levied for occupying military accommodation, but these are more than outweighed by the costs of purchasing furniture. Although this pattern of behaviour does cause financial problems for a minority, it has become overwhelmingly the approach adopted by the majority of Service families, most of whom do not experience unmanageable debt as a result.

Thirdly, all military families confronting living in military housing have to consider a number of aspects concerning its quality. Standards vary enormously, reflecting, primarily, the age of the housing stock. Thus, heating systems, thermal insulation, room and garden sizes are not standardised at all military locations. Families arriving to occupy new married quarters may therefore find them better or worse than previous military housing, but it is unlikely they will find them exactly the same. What they will find the same is the restricted range of colours used for internal decoration.

Qualitative issues also arise in the standards of maintenance applied to military houses, and the ability of maintenance systems to respond promptly. Maintenance budgets have been subjected to predatory raids throughout the history of British married quarters – either by more powerful sections of a Service faced with a cash crisis or to achieve overall economies for the Service as a whole – with the result that 'slippage' has been the norm rather than the exception in refurbishing and maintaining military properties.

Married couples and their families using married quarters therefore have to be content with highly variable quality standards over which they can exercise virtually no control. The principal attractions of military quarters remain as they have always been – the opportunity for couples to continue living together and to develop their marriage on the basis of shared experience rather than through geographically separate existences. A secondary advantage for Service families has been that such housing is relatively cheap – well below the market price of either rented or owner-occupied accommodation. However, families do pay a different sort of price in living in military housing – the inability to ensure standards conforming with their own and an effective loss of control over a significant area of private life. Insofar as housing does provide an arena in which individuals can guarantee certainty and control for themselves in what may otherwise be a disturbing and turbulent world, living in married quarters diminishes this vital housing function by requiring occupants to accept the letting regulations and quality standards of the military landlord.

Fourthly, families departing from married quarters are exposed to the rigours of systems variously described as *handing over* or *marching out* of their houses. These terms refer to the letting conditions which the military landlord imposes as to the standards of cleanliness expected at the end of a lease period. Unlike civilian landlords, the military impose the task of ensuring these cleanliness standards are achieved on to the outgoing occupants rather than employing cleaning agencies. Families failing to reach the designated standards will, in effect, be fined by deductions from the military employee's salary to recoup the cost of any cleaning service which does have to be invoked to remedy such deficiencies identified by the landlord.

Although military households acknowledge the need for certain cleanliness standards so that incoming families can be assured that whatever time of day or night they arrive, the house will be fit for immediate occupation, they will rapidly learn as married quarter users that the cleanliness standards demanded, and the inspection system established by the landlord to check on what has been achieved, vary considerably between different locations. This is hardly surprising since such inspections inevitably involve a good deal of subjective judgement on the part of the scrutineer. But such variability puts families in married quarters at the mercy of what may seem inconsistent appraisals, and therefore weakens the degree to which the married quarter house can also become a personal home. Moreover, where cleanliness inspectors find fault, this is always experienced as a criticism of the house manager – usually the wife – and frequently causes arguments between the couple.

Finally, military families using married quarters have to make decisions at some point about entering the civilian housing world. At what point – if at all – should the option of owner-occupation be seriously examined? The pressures to acquire housing in the civilian world arise from a number of different directions. Imminent discharge at the end of a contract period obviously forces couples to recognise that they will shortly be required to abandon married quarters. But there are other life-stages too where most military families will reflect on their housing choices. Critically, these are where children are approaching 11 years in age and about to enter a new phase in their schooling; and when spouses have reached a point in their own working lives where further geographical movement would seriously damage their career prospects, or even make employment impossible altogether.

GEOGRAPHICAL MOBILITY

The British term 'turbulence' used throughout the UK armed forces to describe the physical relocation of families is in many ways highly appropriate, since it implies and recognises the psychological pressures produced by frequent house moves. Moving rates highly in the Holmes/Rahe Life Event Scale which lists experiences inducing stress. Although the capacity to manage house moves successfully increases with time, families inevitably face the loss of the local familiar environment whenever they are relocated. Of course, there are usually advantages which accrue in the new location and these will often outweigh the losses caused by having to move. Indeed, some military families claim positively to enjoy the opportunity to move regularly and anticipate the next posting eagerly, though the findings of the 1993/4 *Wives Continuous Attitude Survey*, which looks at the opinions of British Army wives suggests this is only a relatively small minority. Asking the question 'How do you find moving?' produced the following response:

Stressful/very stressful	77.5%
Not very/at all stressful	4.6%
All right	17.9%

Moreover, the ability of families to negotiate major change depends on their life-stage, and moving for the first time may be particularly threatening, as Mady W Segal points out in 'The Military and the Family as Greedy Institutions' (*Journal of Armed Forces and Society*, Vol. 13, Fall 1986):

> The most obvious component of geographical mobility is the requirement to move frequently. Less obvious and less often discussed in the literature on military families is the first move, which perhaps calls for the greatest adjustment. Whether a Service member is already married when entering the military or marries later, the spouse's first residence during military service is usually away from home. This has special implications for young enlisted families because it is likely to be the first time that they are away from their families of orientation and long-term friends. In contrast, junior officers are older and have gone to college, often away from home. Similarly officers' spouses are more likely than enlisted spouses to have gone to college . . . *All, however, are geographically separated from their usual interpersonal networks and sources of social support.* (author's emphasis)

Geographical moves to foreign countries obviously pose extra questions for families, but as Mady Segal goes on to point out even domestic relocation can have enormous implications for American military personnel:

> The United States is geographically large compared with most other countries. Therefore, moves generally take a family relatively large distances, making contact with family and friends more difficult. . . . For families with limited resources and/or small children, this can be especially stressful. The physical environment and climate may also be quite different from what the family members are accustomed to. Whatever the type (including size) of the community, some military families will be used to another type. For example, people from rural areas often find large military installations intimidating; they are unaccustomed to living close to neighbours. The regional dialect may also be unfamiliar to them, straining communication with others and possibly making them feel like outsiders. (Ibid.)

Younger people – whether single or married – seem more vulnerable to the effects on personal health of moving. Thus Joseph M Rothberg, examining *Stress and Suicide in the US Army: Effects of Relocation on Service Members' Mental Health*, found no correlation between geographical mobility and suicide for the majority of soldiers, but did discover such a link for the youngest third of the Army population.

In Britain, shorter physical distances impose fewer barriers to maintaining kin contact for mobile military families. Nevertheless, younger and poorer families – particularly without access to cars – can still be seriously deprived of practical day-to-day kin support.

The Brook Family

Able-Seaman James Brook is 20, the same age as his wife Jayne. There are two children: Claire aged 2½ and Tanya aged three months. The couple have been married for 18 months. When they married, Jayne was pregnant but miscarried three months after the wedding. James is not the father of Claire.

James and Jayne married in Plymouth, where Jayne's family live. However, shortly after getting married, James was drafted to a shore-based job at Rosyth (Scotland).

Jayne became pregnant again soon after the miscarriage and Tanya was born at Rosyth. But within a few weeks of her birth, Jayne became miserable and isolated. She missed the support of her family, in particular the help and advice of her mother in coping with Tanya, and she dreaded the prospect of being left on her own with two small children when James went to sea.

Consequently, James was put under a great deal of pressure from Jayne to seek a return draft to Plymouth, although he feared such a request might harm his career ambitions, and did not share his wife's enthusiasm for Plymouth or frequent contact with her mother.

Eventually he sought help from his Divisional Officer (section manager) who authorised a social enquiry from the Naval Personal and Family Service. This recommended returning the Brook family to Plymouth on the grounds that James Brook's commitment to the Royal Navy would be more assured if kin support was regularly available to his wife. The recommendation was accepted.

Older families also find moving causes severe disruption. School-age children have to transfer to new schools, and the lack of standardised curricula across both the UK and the USA can result in gaps or repetition in their education. Moving produces particular problems for adolescents. Defining themselves on the basis of integration with local peer groups, relocation interferes with this construction of their personal identity. And for spouses in employment, moving may well mean the loss of both work and income. Both American and British Service spouses have lower workforce participation rates than their civilian counterparts.

The frequency of house moves depends to some extent on Service and rank. Lower ranked personnel (who are generally therefore younger and more recently married) tend to move more frequently than older and more senior people. Generally throughout the period 1980–93, British Army and Royal Air Force families could expect to move at least once every two years – and many moved more often. US Department of Defense data suggest that 90% of enlisted personnel and a similar proportion of officers moved at least once within a three year period during the second half of the 1970s. UK civilians in comparison face the upheavals of moving only every seven to eight years on average – moreover, civilians normally have more choice over where and when they want to go.

CHILDREN'S EDUCATION

Interruptions to the education of their children generates much anxiety for military parents. Average rates of 'turbulence' mean that a British Service child will attend three or four schools by the age of 11, and thereafter possibly three more before reaching the age of important, nationally recognised public examinations. Moreover, the variation in the curriculum coverage between the States within America, and similar differences between Scotland and England and Wales in the UK presents additional problems. The lack of nationally standardised assessment systems within England itself, where a number of different Examining Boards measure achievements within their own curriculum, constitutes a further complication because subjects taught within each Board's area are not identical, and sometimes not even compatible with those monitored by adjacent Examining Boards.

Despite some research suggesting that British Service children do not, in fact, suffer in terms of educational attainment as the result of frequent geographical moves (Squadron Leader J Firth RAF Study on the *Educational Attainments of Service Children,* 1975), most parents implicitly feel that frequent changes of school are damaging to their children. Undeniably, geographical moves disrupt children's social relationships even if the educational outcome is less disastrous than parents anticipate. The alternative options available to military families anxious to minimise school changes depend on the Service and specific professional role of the employee. Overseas postings offer the possibility of attending Service-provided schools. Such schools aim to provide continuity and curriculum consistency wherever they are located, so that Service personnel whose postings enable their children to attend such schools are guaranteed relative educational stability, even if the children themselves have to attend more than one Service school. Other military parents subject to postings which require moves only within their homeland do not enjoy this facility and therefore have to decide whether to use locally provided schooling wherever they happen currently to be located.

The principal alternative – both for families on overseas postings and those at home – is to buy places in private schools. Many of these in the UK offer residential provision, and married UK Service personnel in certain circumstances receive a publicly funded cash subsidy – the Boarding School Allowance – which provides assistance towards the cost of such schools. However, the majority of families qualifying for this Allowance have to supplement it with substantial additional payments out of disposable income to meet the full cost of private education.

Private residential education does, of course, provide stability and continuity irrespective of parental location, but for many military families not only is such education expensive but culturally alien to them as well. For many British officers in particular there is a family tradition of attending residential schools, but many current Service users of UK boarding schools are non-officers who did not themselves patronise such schools. Sending their children away to school provokes much anguish for them since both they and their children perceive such a practice as child-rejection. A number of military families in the UK thus become reluctant users of private residential schools only because they feel such a choice is marginally less bad than the discontinuities in education which their children would otherwise be subjected to.

SPOUSE EMPLOYMENT

Discussion of the working patterns and employment expectations of military spouses occurs more extensively in Chapter 6. Nevertheless, it is important to recognise the barriers to systematic employment or education and training that are created by military lifestyles.

The Towers Family

Jim Towers is 29 and a Corporal in a Tank Transport Squadron in the British Army. He is approaching the end of a nine-year engagement period and must shortly decide whether to commit himself for a further 13 years, taking him to his maximum career span as a non-commissioned officer of 22 years. He enjoys the Army, is good at his job and has excellent promotion prospects, including a substantial chance of becoming commissioned. However, because he has been trained by the Army to drive Heavy Goods Vehicles, he also has qualifications which provide him with good employment prospects in civilian life too.

But Jim faces a conflict of interests between his career ambitions and those of his partner. Valerie Towers is 27 and in the two years in which she has been married to Jim she has already moved house three times. Valerie currently works as a receptionist at the local medical centre, but her objective is to qualify as a teacher. She has just been offered a place at a nearby college to train as a teacher starting in the forthcoming autumn. However, the course extends over three years and Valerie is aware that in the normal course of events, Jim will be moved at least once during that period. Valerie wants some stability to enable her to fulfil her own career goals, and has made it clear to Jim that taking up the opportunity now offered to her and qualifying as a teacher is so important that she will refuse to accompany him if he is posted away from the area during the next three years.

Jim makes some enquiries and discovers that his wife's training course does not constitute a reason why the Army might be willing to delay his next posting. As Jim has seen a number of military marriages collapse because the partners lived apart in 'voluntary separation', he is unwilling to risk his marriage in this way, and so decided not to re-engage.

The inability of the employer to be flexible in this instance cost the continuing services of a qualified staff member – trained, at considerable expense, by the Army. Many military marriages face similar crunch points where spouses assert their own need for recognition and their right to pursue their own careers. And many Service employees have been faced with dissatisfied partners presenting them with the choice: do you want me or the Army/Navy/Air Force? Thus the abnormal difficulties of constructing dual-career households in the military engender extra marital stress.

TEMPORARY SEPARATIONS

Periods spent apart are normal for the partners in military marriages. Unaccompanied deployments, whether on land or sea, constitute the longest and most obvious forms of separation. But military institutions require their members to be permanently updated in their professional skills, and so separation resulting from attendance at training courses is also very common. Moreover, skills acquired have to be practised, and so exercises enabling tactics, personnel and equipment to be used and assessed are also frequent. Additionally, the round-the-clock nature of military life means that even when a couple are living together, work patterns may involve unsocial hours and so reduce the time that family members can actually spend together.

Unsurprisingly, the majority of British Army wives sampled in 1993/4 agreed with the following statement: 'I feel that I am able to cope when my husband is away on unaccompanied tours'. This produced the following response:

Agree/strongly agree	65.8%
Neither agree nor disagree	19.3%
Disagree/strongly disagree	14.9%

A good deal of dissatisfaction was, however, expressed with the quality and availability of support provided by the Army for temporarily separated households.

As with geographical turbulence, the impact of separation on marriages and families depends on when it occurs in the history of the relationship. Separation is clearly found more disturbing by young wives, for whom the departure of a husband brings about their first experience of living in a house alone. The additional responsibility is sometimes frightening and unwelcome. Where the separation occurs early in a new marriage, it also interrupts the important process of constructing a new relationship, for which the couple self-evidently need to be together. When the partner remaining behind is not only young but also required to assume full responsibility for children, it is not difficult to understand why anxiety levels rise.

More mature marriages learn how to manage separations successfully and the prospect of a further period apart becomes less frightening for the couple, though still normally unwelcome.

> You shall be together when the white wings of
> death scatter your days.
> Aye, you shall be together even in the silent
> memory of God.
>> But let there be spaces in your togetherness
>> And let the winds of heaven dance between you
> Love one another but make not a bond of love.
> Fill each other's cup but drink not from one cup.
> Give one another of your bread but eat not
> of the same loaf
> Sing and dance together and be joyous, but let
> each one of you be alone

Even as the strings of a lute are alone though
they quiver with the same music.

(from *The Prophet* by Khalil Gibran)

More prosaically, it is clear that self-esteem and personal development can be enhanced through periods of separation. But for this to happen, the couple need to understand and negotiate the dynamics of the situation. Effective separation management involves prior planning:

* what domestic roles will be assumed by the remaining partner?
* what financial arrangements will apply during the separation?
* how will the couple stay in touch with each other during the separation?
* how will the return of the absentee be managed?

Undoubtedly the two key problem areas are the *role switching* which is enforced by the absence of one partner, and issues arising from the *return and reintegration* of the absentee.

All households have to decide on appropriate demarcation in managing essential tasks. These include house management, child care, overseeing gardens and cars, and earning money. Such roles are normally shared between family members reflecting their particular competences. The temporary absence of one partner obliges the remaining partner to adopt all these roles. Initially this may be undertaken reluctantly and with a high degree of apprehension. With practice, military marriages swing into accustomed – but changed – routines when the Service employee is absent. Over time, however, regular separation affects role demarcation, reducing the contribution and power within the household of the absentee. Far from the apprehension which accompanied the initial separation, the partner remaining may begin to relish the certainty and control which being the only adult present in the household permits. Mealtimes, and menus, can be decided without consultation; children are unable to challenge behaviour rules by appealing to another adult; and the financial circumstances are often known with greater clarity.

It is not difficult to see, therefore, why problems can sometimes arise over the reallocation of roles when the absentee returns. Sometimes the waiting partner has developed such confidence and expertise in managing all domestic roles that the returner feels redundant, as the story of the Stephens family illustrates.

The Stephens Family

Major John Stephens is 37. His wife Anne is 39. With their two children Lucy (9) and Susie (7), the Stephens have just arrived in Germany together as a family after an unaccompanied tour for John in Northern Ireland, during which time Anne and the children lived in their own house in England.

Anne has sought help from the Army welfare support system because she has discovered that her husband has been having an affair while in Ireland. John has admitted this is true, but stated he hopes the accompanied posting will enable them to grow back together as a couple. However, John retains photos of his lover, writes to her and telephones occasionally as well.

Anne has delivered an ultimatum to her husband: all contact with the other woman must cease immediately if he wishes the Stephens household to remain united. She is a determined, forceful, articulate and highly competent person who has become used to making all important decisions in the household – Anne decided on the house that they bought; she renegotiated the leasing agreement on the family car; she decided on where the children should go to school; and she has taken sole responsibility for all aspects of the household's financial dealings. This position of dominance in the relationship is not entirely of her own choice: it was enforced because of her husband's many absences on duty. Nevertheless, demonstrating that she is a highly efficient household manager provides Anne with considerable personal satisfaction.

It is easy to see here how John Stephens has felt himself increasingly excluded from this household, redundant largely except for his financial input. To compensate for this, he has begun a relationship to which his contributions are valued and which recreates his sense of status and significance. The origins of these destructive forces within the Stephens marriage lay in their faulty planning and management of separation. Neither adult appeared to have recognised the hazards involved in role switching or to have the ability to construct a system of mutually acceptable roles when they were together. The Stephens divorced.

Military marriages confront a variety of temporary separations, in fact, which vary in terms of length, the degree of perceived risk for the absentee and the amount of advance warning which the couple receive. Unexpected separations – which may occur because of unpredictable military engagements such as the 1991 Gulf War – more frequently arise as the result of illness or accident necessitating the replacement of Service personnel at short notice. Deployments of this kind interrupt planned family activities – such as children's birthdays – and exacerbate the sense of insecurity and lack of control over life which afflicts many military families. Such separations are difficult to plan for.

Some separations are rather euphemistically described as 'voluntary'. These occur when partners agree to live apart temporarily, not because accompaniment is impossible, but to meet the employment needs of the spouse or to enable children to continue their education without changing schools. Some relationships collapse under these pressures, often because the return of the absentee is less idyllic than had been anticipated. This is particularly noticeable in marriages where the couple choose to live apart during the week reuniting at weekends.

The Simpson Family

When Alan Simpson joined the Royal Navy, he chose Portsmouth as his 'base port'. This was because he could normally expect to be located there when not at sea. However, changes in the pattern of employment in his particular trade mean that he now works normally at Plymouth – one hundred miles distant – when on land. Alan and his wife Margaret bought a house in Portsmouth, Margaret works there and the children go to Portsmouth schools. Moving to Plymouth is something the Simpsons decided against.

Alan normally arrives home by 6 pm on Fridays, but has to

leave again on Sunday evenings. Ironically, on his journey home, he passes colleagues driving in the opposite direction but also engaged in an identical Monday–Friday routine.

This pattern has continued for about 12 months, and Alan expects to stay at least as long again at his current post. However, the marriage is suffering. Far from the weekends bringing the couple closer together or being experienced as second honeymoons, Alan has begun to dread returning home. Tired and drained at the end of the week, he wants nothing more than to relax in his own home. But Margaret has been there all week, trapped by her parenting role, and her urgent need is for adult company and joint social activities. The children too persistently compete for Alan's attention, and the list of minor household tasks demanding action seems to get ever longer.

Because he has become increasingly disillusioned about the weekends and finds them periods of considerable conflict, Alan has chosen to return home late on Fridays so that he can be fairly certain the children will be in bed and it will be too late to go out socialising with Margaret.

Unless the Simpsons can recognise the conflicting needs the adults have of each other at weekends and develop strategies to resolve them, the marriage is obviously at risk. Even though separation may be for relatively short periods and chosen by the couple themselves, it produces change within the previously established structure of the relationships which must be addressed.

The home to which he returns is by no means the home he left, or the home which he recalled or longed for during his absence . . . and the homecomer is not the same man who left. He is neither the same for himself, nor for those who await his return.

(Arnold Schuetz, *The Homecomer*;
American Journal of Science 1945)

These observations relate to American Servicemen returning after the Second World War, often after prolonged periods of separation. Nevertheless, what is expressed here is true in some degree for all separations, whatever the length and whether chosen or enforced. Change occurs within the home while one partner is absent – children grow older, rooms are redecorated, partners enter new employment – and so the home remembered by the absentee becomes to some extent a figment of nostalgia. And the absent partner also undergoes new experiences which cannot be easily and quickly shared with the spouse. The absentee also becomes in some senses a different person, and may experience personality changes which do not fit comfortably with the spouse. The rash of divorces in the British Army after the Gulf War bears witness to this, as does the study 'The Families of US Navy Prisoners of War from Vietnam Five Years after Reunion' (D Stephen Nice *et al.*, *Journal of Marriage and the Family*; May 1981) which found that the post-repatriation divorce rate among returned prisoners of war was significantly higher than for a control group.

ACCOMPANIED OVERSEAS DEPLOYMENTS

Opportunities for foreign travel have in the past figured quite highly in the motivation of armed forces recruits. The logistics of superpower confrontation during the Cold War era required many American and British military personnel to serve abroad, and the apparent permanence of some of these locations allowed for accompanied postings and the establishment of national educational, medical and commercial support systems.

Partners and other dependants were thus also able to experience life overseas. As with all geographical turbulence, foreign moves entail the loss of the known and familiar surroundings, but proffer the adventure of a new country, different climate and cultural variety. Support systems for military families overseas have received more priority and resources than at home, so although relocating abroad has some frightening dimensions, community integration and assistance systems have generally enabled incomers to adjust rapidly to the nuances of overseas life and to feel a sense of belonging – admittedly to an expatriate society – which often provides a stronger sense of group identity than military families feel in their own countries.

The attractiveness of foreign deployments for families is obviously affected by where they are. Hong Kong, Cyprus or Germany – the major venues for accompanied British service – each have different advantages and drawbacks. The more exotic and distant destinations are attractive to many simply for those reasons. Others find the humidity unexpected and intolerable, and the distance from extended family members causes serious concern in the event of illness in the home country. Decisions about spousal careers and children's education have to be made in just the same way with overseas accompanied postings as they do with internal moves. The repercussions of this form of turbulence are very similar to those discussed above. One major difference is that for British and American Services alike, the prospects for spouses of obtaining paid employment appropriate to their educational and professional attainments are severely curtailed by moving abroad. Where work can be attained, it is frequently menial and poorly paid.

Summary

This Chapter has examined a number of features of military life which differ either in kind or degree from civilian society and which have important consequences for military marriages.

Six such *endogenous* factors have been identified – accommodation; geographic mobility; children's education; employment opportunities for spouses; separations; and overseas postings. Although none of these issues is unique to military families, their cumulative effect is undeniably more onerous than the pressures their civilian counterparts have to contend with. Moreover, many of these concerns must be faced not only more often than is the case for civilians, but by markedly younger populations inevitably lacking much life experience.

To what extent do military families themselves have insight into the effect that armed forces membership has on their marriages? The British Army's *Continuous Attitude Surveys*, both for wives and serving personnel, invites reflection on the impact of Army life on marriage and family life. Asked to respond to the statement: 'I have often experienced personal problems with my marriage that are related to my husband being in the Army', a sample of 1,407 wives divided as follows:

Agree/strongly agree	38.8%
Neither agree nor disagree	14.0%
Disagree/strongly disagree	47.1%

(*Wives Continuous Attitude Survey*, November 1993–March 1994,
S J E Smith and A Hampson; Army Personnel
Research Establishment, 1994)

A group of married Army officers of similar size produced these responses to questions concerned with the outcome of Army life on their marriages:

The effects on the stability of family life in general

Very or fairly satisfied	20.7%
Neutral	36.9%
Very or fairly dissatisfied	42.5%

The effects on your marriage

Very or fairly satisfied	32.4%
Neutral	44.6%
Very or fairly dissatisfied	23.0%

The effects on children's education

Very or fairly satisfied	19.8%
Neutral	27.0%
Very or fairly dissatisfied	53.1%

The effects on spouse's career

Very or fairly satisfied	8.7%
Neutral	21.4%
Very or fairly dissatisfied	69.%

(*Officers Continuous Attitude Survey*, January–June 1993;
Army Personnel Research Establishment, 1993)

It is evident from these *Attitude Surveys* that both serving personnel and spouses identify significant marital pressures which arise from membership of the armed forces. But these represent merely the endogenous factors specific to military life. In the next Chapter, the reverberations of these particular tensions will be examined in the context of those additional, exogenous challenges to marital stability which all relationships have to successfully overcome if they are to survive.

CHAPTER 4

Divorce and the Armed Forces

Divorce became much more common in the last quarter of the twentieth century in all western societies. Britain displayed a particularly rapid increase in divorce petitions as the following table shows.

Divorce: Final Decrees (United Kingdom) (Thousands)

1961	1971	1981	1992
27	79	157	175

(Source: *Social Trends Number 25;* HMSO 1995)

The 1992 figures implied a divorce rate in England and Wales of 12.9 per 1,000 married people. In Scotland, the rate was slightly lower at 11.5. Overall, the United Kingdom entered the decade with the highest marriage breakdown rate in Europe, equalled only by Denmark.

Rather more memorably, what these statistics mean is that one British marriage in three can be expected to break down and end in divorce before reaching its 15-year point, and for some social groups, particularly the very young and the unemployed the risk factor exceeds 50% – in effect, divorce is more likely than not to occur. The dramatic jump in divorce petitions in England and Wales in the early 1970s reflected legal changes ushered in by the 1969 Divorce Reform Act which permitted divorce on the basis of irretrievable marriage breakdown – as declared by the partners in the relationship – and dispensed with juridical insistence for supporting evidence from third parties which had often been costly to accumulate. Undeniably, changes in the law have facilitated divorce in Britain since 1969. The argument that such changes *caused* the escalating divorce rate is disputed below.

British experience has been paralleled throughout much of Western Europe and in the United States too.

USA: Ratio of Marriages – Divorces 1960–92 (Millions)

	Marriages	Divorces	Divorces as % Marriages
1960	1.5	0.4	27%
1970	2.2	0.7	32%
1980	2.4	1.2	50%
1992	2.4	1.2	50%

(Source: *Statistical Abstract* of the United States 1994)

A powerful combination of economic shifts – especially in the proportion of women engaging in the labour force and in rising male unemployment – together with attitudinal changes towards marriage, arising in particular from feminist challenges and from an awareness of the increased possibilities for individuals to exercise personal choice and leave failing relationships, have all subjected the socially approved model of monogamous lifelong marriage to one partner to fierce attacks.

The concept of 'love' being a sufficient motive force to sustain a lifelong relationship needs drastic surgery in our culture. We should encourage the perception of marriage as a mutual commitment to a domestic partnership of bed and board. This might seem unromantic but should encourage the partners to reflect the material basis and role exchanges on which the relationship is grounded. Preparation for marriage education should in consequence lay great stress on how the worlds of work, money and the unpaid domestic and household economy underpin successful marriages, stress the severe interruptions caused by children, and examine in practical detail the daily marriage timetable in terms of role demarcation both where the partners are in paid employment and where they are not.

(from 'Conclusions' in *Divorce Matters* by J Burgoyne,
R Ormrod and M Richards; London: Penguin, 1987)

In western societies, marriages are based largely on personal choice of partner. Pre-marital education is received only by a minority of people, and enabling individuals to make appropriate partner choices does not form a standard part of the secondary school or college curriculum. Even where such assistance is provided and potential partners are invited to explore some of the prosaic features of life outlined above to enable them to make compatible choices, there is still one very significant dimension missing from the equation – that of time, and the imponderable consequences for a relationship which flow from its projected existence over very long periods.

One of the less recognised features of the twentieth century is the increase in the actual or potential length of marriage that has been brought about because of steady improvements in public health services, water quality and the virtual eradication of previously fatal infectious diseases. In Britain these developments have virtually doubled the possible duration of a marriage in less than a century. A couple of good health and marrying at average ages in the late 1890s could hope to spend 25–30 years together before death ended the relationship. During this period, the wife could anticipate some 12–14 years of pregnancy and the management of infants under the age of three. Depending on her social class and the housing and other economic circumstances she enjoyed, between one-quarter and two-thirds of all her pregnancies would fail to produce a child still living one year after its date of birth. And the risks to mothers of dying in or subsequent to childbirth through infection were high.

In contrast, a couple marrying in the UK in the 1990s – again assuming average health and ages – can anticipate a potential marriage of 56 years. Thus the Golden Wedding becomes an attainable objective for all. During this time, the wife will spend perhaps eight years either pregnant or in charge of an infant under three. The phase of intensive care and nurturing of very young children is thus reduced to one-seventh of the possible marriage length, and obviously undermines the practicality of one or both the parents viewing the nurturing and socialising of children as a full-time task occupying a major proportion of the marriage. Since it is preponderantly women in Western societies who have been expected to provide the care and sustenance of children, it is particularly women who have been affected by the dramatic reduction in the time necessarily devoted to the management of very young children in twentieth-century marriages. The remarkable expansion of married women into the workforce, particularly since the Second World War, has thus reflected not only the needs of national economies for additional non-male labour, but also the requirements of women themselves to evolve roles external to the home to replace the earlier drudgery of incessant infant care.

This extended timespan for contemporary marriages introduces one of the *exogenous factors* influencing its nature and continuation. During a partnership period which can be expected to endure for over 50 years, an array of significant life-events can be expected to occur. Some of these will reflect *choices* actually made by the couple themselves – such as to marry, to become parents, and in the allocation of domestic and non-domestic roles. Other events will *impose* themselves – these may include illness, disability, unemployment and bereavement. All such experiences dictate change for the individuals and relationship concerned, but predicting many years ahead how somebody will respond to major life-events – and whether that reactions will be compatible with the partner – is impossible. However pragmatic pre-marital education seeks to be, therefore, it cannot realistically address future change of an unknown nature. In part this is because the character behaviour and attitudes of the individuals who will be obliged to address change in the future is itself very difficult to forecast. People are altered by events in their lives, and in a meaningful sense do not remain the *same* person throughout their lives. Although a central core of memories and a unique personal history helps to define us both to ourselves and others, our competencies, expectations and ambitions are subtly amended as we grow older. In a very real sense, a person of 40 is not identical with that person when 20. Yet a couple embarking on a late twentieth century marriage are entering a commitment which, by its very nature of lying in the future, is largely unforseeable.

Not surprisingly, modern commentaries on marriage which acknowledge the significance of its vastly extended length question the ability of the socially approved model of the monogamous, lifelong relationship to provide a practical and attainable standard.

FACTORS AFFECTING MARITAL CONTINUATION

The last Chapter examined specific features of military communities which influenced armed forces marriages. In addition to the unique combination of circumstances which military marriages have to negotiate, they have to confront and overcome as well all those exogenous factors found in contemporary societies which pose threats to lifelong relationships. Apart from the potential longevity of modern marriage, other such key matters are:-

* the expectations about *roles and rules* which the individual partners bring into their relationship;
* the reappraisal of self and partner incorporated in the popular but imprecise term *mid-life crisis*;
* the extension of the idea of *obsolescence* to personal relationships from the economic world of the market place and advertising;
* the *differential rates of marital satisfaction* experienced by the partners in a relationship; and
* developments external to the marriage affecting *employment patterns* for one or both of the partners.

All these factors are moderated too by social class and ethnicity.

ROLES, RULES AND LIVING HAPPILY EVER AFTER

Two people marrying do not automatically share identical expectations about role performance and demarcation within their new relationship. Deriving from two different families of origin, each individual accumulates differing perceptions about appropriate adult role behaviour within marriage. Kin – especially parents – are likely to form the dominant influence in establishing models of behaviour. This is the marriage which most people know best and replicating behavioural patterns observed in that marriage is often what individuals expect to do when they themselves get married. A minority of people marrying will do so from a background affected by divorce or the death of a parent, or will come from unstable families and have experienced periods in care or in foster homes. But whatever the degree of solidity and continuity individuals have experienced in their own families, they are all exposed also to media images of marriage which may or may not conform to their own expectations. A couple marrying at present cannot avoid realising that a great variety of marital styles exist, and that role allocation and demarcation between them allows for an element of personal choice rather than being irremediably preordained by church, government or family background.

The movement towards symmetrical marriages, with an equality of role-sharing both within and outside the home, was discussed in the previous Chapter. Whilst progress towards a complete equality of responsibility for roles external to the household – predominantly money-earning – and internal roles – mainly house and child maintenance – has been modest (and, indeed, some feminist critics would deny *any* such change has occurred at all), in many marriages changing patterns of employment opportunities have dictated that wives and mothers work outside the home. Normally this has been *as well as* their husbands, but sometimes *instead of* – particularly in geographical areas where structural change has decimated traditional mining or manufacturing industries.

Cultural changes also influence marriage roles. Concepts of *fairness* and *justice* have undoubtedly come to be applied to modern relationships in ways which challenge many of the role models provided by families of origin. Claiming to want to share tasks equally in marriage characterises young never-married people in Britain, and although subsequent practice may belie this intention, there is certainly pressure generated within the relationship to reject the strictly segregated set of roles demonstrated by the parents of couples marrying today.

Not only is there more choice about the allocation of marital roles, and therefore more opportunity for dispute and conflict, attitudes towards rules and how decisions about them should be made may also fail to coincide closely. Studies examining domestic violence show repeatedly that it is the failure of one partner to conform to a rule (often imposed unilaterally and without debate) by the other which triggers violence. Edicts about meals – what they will consist of on specific days, or the precise times at which they will be available – provide fruitful territory for disagreement. Failure to comply with the demand about the content or timing of meals is perceived as mutiny demanding instant punishment. For what is being challenged here is not only the outcome of the rule, but the right of one partner to dictate this particular rule at all.

How couples make decisions about rule-making has received relatively little investigation. It seems evident that in practice the respective skill levels and the roles which it has been mutually agreed each individual should play influence what actually happens in the relationship. Thus, decisions on where items of furniture shall be placed in the home appear to be made far more frequently by wives than either jointly or by husbands. The only areas of the home which husbands routinely control in terms of deciding what is located there turn out to be relatively peripheral areas such as garages, workshops, or cellars. The underlying – if unacknowledged – reason for this is clear – the physical distribution of furniture and household goods affects the task of cleaning. Since this still falls predominantly to female partners in heterosexual relationships, the right to make rules about the distribution of household items is accepted by both partners as belonging to the wife. Similarly, the partner possessing the superior cooking skills usually decides the organisation and content of the kitchen.

Disputes about rules are often unrecognised as such by the couple concerned. What *they* perceive themselves to be arguing about is something much more immediate – the timing of a meal or the failure of one of them to buy some needed household object. But underlying this in reality is a dispute about *who* is entitled to make the rules which will determine these activities. Particular difficulties about rule making and conforming can arise in military families where the Service employee has a senior role which incorporates an institutional entitlement to make rules which inform the professional lives of others, and who then applies this in the domestic arena as well.

The Clarke Family

Appointed Regimental Sergeant Major 18 months ago, Alan Clarke (age 38) is justifiably proud of his successful Army career, which began as a Junior Leader 20 years ago. He has achieved his ultimate goal: RSM and therefore 'First Soldier of the Regiment' status. Now there is an excellent prospect of being commissioned and becoming an officer in the near future, and so a chance to extend his Army career, which would otherwise come to an end in two years' time.

Alan Clarke has always driven himself hard. He feels attention to detail, unfailing punctuality and reliability, and 100% commitment to the Army are vital ingredients in his success. These are virtues he strives hard to inculcate in others, together with a high standard of physical fitness, which he maintains for himself.

Jean Clarke, his wife, who is aged 34, is a qualified physiotherapist, but has been unable to practise her profession at Alan's current station. She is proud of her husband's achievements, but is increasingly restless with Alan's refusal to recognise that there is a world beyond the Army. His reluctance to discuss his eventual discharge from the Army worries her.

Last month whilst RSM Clarke was away from home on exercise, Tony Clarke (age 16) stole a tracksuit from a local sports shop. He was identified from a security camera video. Utterly distraught, Mrs Clarke returned the goods and managed to persuade the shopkeeper not to prosecute. When Alan Clarke returned home, he stood Tony to attention and gave him a hell of a talking to about honesty, integrity, and how family misbehaviour at this critical time could severely damage Alan's chance of being commissioned.

Tony received his GCSE results three days ago: they are disappointing and it seems he will have to return to school to retake these exams next year. Two days after these results, Jean found Tony lying on his bed with cuts to both wrists. As Alan had the car at work, Jean got a neighbour to drive Tony to hospital, where he is currently an in-patient. His physical damage, fortunately, is minimal.

With much soul-searching, RSM Clarke has reluctantly agreed to seek advice from the Families Welfare Officer – somebody he has known over many years. Alan wants to know what he should do to make his family stay calm and supportive at this important time – after all, a family problem like this cannot increase his chances of getting a commission. Surely Jean and Tony should be able to see the need to be disciplined and supportive? But Jean is apparently very angry with Alan, and has even threatened to leave him unless he stops putting the Army first. However, Alan believes that putting the Army first is exactly what has to be done to secure the welfare of the entire family – but Jean and Tony just seem so short-sighted and unable to accept this.

What Alan Clarke wants from the Welfare System is advice on how to get the other members of the family to see reason.

This is not an uncommon situation in military households. Key age-points for promotion often coincide with children reaching adolescence and demonstrating their first tentative moves towards independence. For personnel professionally required to make rules which govern the daily life and working environment of other staff, leaving the parade ground behind when returning home can be difficult. It is especially galling for such individuals – who can legitimately demand that others exhibit order and control – to have publicly exposed disorder and a lack of control in their own families.

MID-LIFE CRISES

In the middle of the journey of their lives, the majority of couples must confront a dismaying variety of demands and dilemmas.

. . . The partners in the relationship are undergoing a complex process of summing up their individual lives and shared past and are imagining themselves forward with a newly diminished sense of how much time lies before them.

(*Intimate Partners: Patterns in Love and Marriage*, Maggie Scarfe, London: Century Hutchinson, 1987).

'Mid-life crisis' is not necessarily a universal experience, nor an unambiguous descriptive term. Popularly, it refers to a process of *personal reappraisal* which many people undoubtedly do undergo at some stage between 35 and 50. What is examined, often silently, are the goals and values which have previously characterised their lives. How realistic have these become? What employment ambitions will be realised? What personal and family aims have been achieved?

Personal reassessments of this kind are often triggered by a development which obliges an individual to reflect on their career objectives and probable outcomes. In many occupations – and certainly in the armed forces – there is a close relationship between age and hierarchical level. If a specified stage has not been reached by a particular chronological age, then further advancement is improbable or restricted. Failure to achieve an organisation's age-stage requirements inevitably induces some sense of loss, but in time energies that have been thwarted within the employment framework may be diverted and directed outside instead. Thus, sporting, civic or social goals will replace ambitions denied at work. Alternative sources of life satisfaction are identified to confirm the individual's self-esteem and sense of purpose.

Such a process of inner deliberation does produce a person who, in important respects, *has become significantly different*. However, this process of self-appraisal extends not only to the world of work, but to friendships, social roles and to marriage itself. Is this relationship still appropriate? Do the attitudes, expectations, values and behaviour of the partner fit with the individual who has emerged from reassessment? What kind of partner *would* match the revised values and life-plans which have resulted? Inevitably, therefore this process of introspection includes a critique of the quality and suitability of the marriage – although this is, of course, equally true for the partner, who may be undergoing a similar experience of reappraisal.

In the armed forces, 'mid-life crisis' can be induced by the coincidence of key life-stages – the departure of children from the family home, and the ending of a Service career demanding the return to the civilian environment.

The Buckingham Family

George Buckingham (aged 42) is a Warrant Officer in the British Army. He has been married to Margaret (aged 44) for 23 years, and they have two children aged 21 and 19, the younger of whom has just left home to become a university student.

Margaret Buckingham has sought counselling support through the Army Welfare Office. George is due to leave the Army next year but is refusing to make any civilian plans, hoping instead to be retained in a subordinate role on the 'Long Service List'. The competition to stay in the Service from colleagues of similar age and experience is intense, and George's chances of remaining in the Army are less than 1:10. Nevertheless, according to Margaret, George refuses to produce any fall-back plan for civilian life should his Army ambitions fail. As a result, Margaret is very worried about what their future housing and employment prospects will be. George has refused to seek advice from the Resettlement Service – which assists military employees back into the civilian world – and is spending most evenings in the Sergeants Mess drinking in order to avoid being confronted with Margaret's anxieties when he returns home.

Margaret appears to have accepted for herself that a key stage in her life has finished – that of nurturing the children at home. She has undertaken training courses in word-processing and office management and is keen to offer her newly acquired skills in the employment market. She appears also to have acknowledged that life with the Army is ending too. She sees George as wilfully refusing to recognise that Army life must come to an end at some time, adopting an ostrich-position which threatens the future for both of them. Margaret has undertaken a personal reappraisal and conceived an acceptable plan for herself. George's denial of their current reality and his refusal to look forward has forced Margaret to concede that there might be substantial disadvantages in remaining with George – and that a future without him could be necessary.

In this instance, the Army Welfare Office established that Buckingham was not to be retained in the Service. Faced with this unwelcome reality, George reluctantly engaged in the Resettlement process. They were successfully assisted in finding civilian accommodation after leaving their Army house. Margaret Buckingham obtained employment quite soon after her husband's discharge, but George did not. They did, however, remain married.

OBSOLESCENCE AND PERSONAL RELATIONSHIPS

All members of Western societies are exposed to advertising pressures which market new goods by asserting that those already in our possession have become out of date. It is implied that our obligations to ourselves, other family members or social status therefore demand that the obsolete item be replaced. It is not surprising, therefore, that the evaluation of partners and marital partnerships is conducted similarly in the language we are familiar with in assessing whether the washing-machine has become outmoded.

The dramatic acceleration in divorce – especially in Britain – since 1970 has produced voices critical of divorce legislation which has undeniably made the process simpler. But has legislation facilitating the ending of marriages actually precipitated the rapid rise in divorce? Colin Gibson thinks not:

Structural modification in the form of government family policy, increasing female employment opportunity and better wages have created improved financial support for lone wives and mothers. All this has allowed wives greater (but not equal) freedom and ability to choose whether they wish to continue an unhappy marriage or seek divorce. *It has been these social transformations which have helped create the patterns and numbers of divorce rather than reform of divorce grounds.* [Author's italics]

(Colin Gibson, *Dissolving Wedlock*; Routledge, 1994, p. 173)

Gibson goes on to suggest that, ironically, it is precisely the exercise of *personal choice* – much vaunted by conservative critics of contemporary divorce statistics – which is the underlying factor.

> We live in an ambivalent enterprise and free-market culture of individualism in which the licence of choice dominates. The Soviet Union and its allied states have crumbled before the ideology of free democratic self-determination. The provision of choice allows far more citizens to examine and consider what they expect of either the government or their marriage . . . Within a regime of open divorce and against a social ethos of self-fulfilment, every day provides a fresh spousal opportunity to re-examine the barometer of personal marital felicity.
>
> (Gibson *ibid.*, p. 214)

Where individual analysis by one partner in a marriage results in the conclusion that a future together is likely to be worse rather than better, the decision to terminate such a redundant relationship is given justification by the free-market notion of obsolescence. What right-minded contemporary consumer would choose to remain in a relationship predicted to be for worse? Although the wider society may perceive there to be benefit from couples staying together through thick and thin, such an alleged advantage of *social stability* does not accrue to the unhappy couple but to the population as a whole. Once it is recognised that social controls over marriage breakdown have been imposed historically by church and state to dictate approved patterns of marriage and child production, those who are unhappily married will challenge and overthrow controls which require them to endure personal suffering in the interests of society at large. The concepts of obsolescence and personal choice induce an awareness that traditional views about the nature and purpose of marriage have themselves become out of date and deny the ultimate right of choice in marriage partnerships.

DIFFERENTIAL RATES OF MARITAL SATISFACTION

It seems likely that greater freedom to choose and, if necessary, to live independently of male partners has encouraged women generally to become less tolerant of marriages which they find unsatisfactory. A number of studies on marital satisfaction have suggested that men benefit more than women. (See, for example, J Bernard *The Future of Marriage*; London: Penguin, 1976, which reviews North American research; and *Who Divorces?* by B Thornes and J Collard; London: Routledge, 1979, which established links within the UK between age, socio-economic group membership and divorce.) Feminist approaches have suggested that marriage, while beneficial to the mental health of men, is damaging to that of women, and that the pattern of segregated male and female roles typically found in pre-1960 British and American marriages was designed to ensure the continued subordination of women within an institution – marriage – structured to reflect and perpetuate male supremacy within the wider society outside the home.

Bernard has drawn attention to the differing perceptions about the nature of a marriage held by the partners involved. Overwhelmingly, women report marriage to be a less satisfactory experience than their husbands. Often, indeed, the couple appear not be to describing the same marriage at all, and, in an important sense, they *are* reporting on different marriages. The husband's marriage is generally perceived by him to be satisfactory and advantageous. The wife's marriage is different – less emotionally rewarding, and sometimes problematic in the roles resulting from the attribution of the term wife.

Part of this discrepancy arises from the expectation widely held in Western society that women adjust naturally – even instinctively – to motherhood. In reality, parenting comes no more naturally to women than to men, but the social presumption that women will exhibit rapid bonding with babies and manage their nurturing with ease and aplomb causes intense guilt and depression for those women for whom such successful mothering proves unattainable.

We see so many couples whose difficulties can be traced back to when they first became parents. The baby was planned, yet the experience of parenthood has been a volcanic eruption.
(To Have and To Hold: Marriage and the First Baby,
Christopher Clulow; University of Aberdeen Press.)

WHO IS MOST LIKELY TO DIVORCE?

Given the specific pressures applied to military marriages in addition to social trends which have generated a rapid rise in divorce, it is not surprising to find some evidence suggesting that marriage breakdown rates are higher in the armed forces than in the civilian world. In the UK, SSAFA (Soldiers, Sailors and Airmen's Family Association), a charitable body which combines the provision of professional social work and health visiting services for the Ministry of Defence on a contract basis to British military communities overseas with financial and other forms of support to veterans, claimed in November 1993 that the prevailing marriage breakdown rate in the British Army was more than double the United Kingdom average. The early 1990s undeniably constituted a particularly difficult period for British armed forces, with enforced redundancies produced by defence expenditure cuts coinciding with stressful engagements in the Gulf War and in the service of the United Nations. Such pressures could be expected to take an additional toll of Service marriages.

In contrast, some American research does not support a linkage between being a member of a military community and above-average marriage breakdown rates. J W Croakes and R S Lyon, writing in *The International Journal of the Sociology of the Family* (1979) under the title 'Factors Related to Tours of Duty and Marital Adjustment' reported on the experiences of 133 Warrant Officers. They concluded that the marital satisfaction of this sample did not appear to be influenced by the number of unaccompanied overseas tours. Of course, such a subject group by definition represents only older and more experienced members of American military communities – battle-hardened survivors whose ability to absorb successfully separation from their families provides no evidence about younger and more vulnerable relationships at lower rank levels. A study of *The Relationship between Army Life and the Family Life of Soldiers* undertaken by J C Woelfel in *The Review of Public Data Use* (1979) investigated the effects of selected Army experiences – such as separation, geographical mobility and fringe benefits such as health care services – on the declared rate of marital satisfaction of 116 married soldiers (79 male, 37 female) and on their intentions to remain in the Army. No statistically significant relationship between these selected experiences of US Army life and marriage breakdown was observed. The soldiers did, however, rate separation (negatively) and housing and health care (positively) in their re-enlistment decisions.

Incontrovertible data indicting military employment as a cause of marriage breakdown do not exist. Indeed, some British Army and Royal Air Force divorce statistics suggest that Service marital breakdown rates may well be lower than the national average, at least for specific years. This may be a reflection of higher educational levels and deferred marriage age – both of which correlate with lower marital breakdown rates – or a tribute to counselling and occupational welfare support systems which assist couples to manage and overcome their problems, or, perhaps more probably, it may reflect the differential rates of occupation of military housing within the British armed forces. What is clear is that divorces which occur after the conclusion of military employment are not recorded in Defence statistics, even though the origins of marital difficulties may lie in the period spent in the Services. Within military communities, some pessimistic commentators express astonishment that military divorce rates are not even higher than those published in view of the combination of endogenous and exogenous threats to which Service marriages are steadily exposed.

Paradoxically, the very provision of Service housing which can be criticised as inciting marriage amongst very young couples with extremely limited courtship patterns may also constitute a barrier to divorce. Where a marriage breaks down and the couple concerned occupy military housing, the resulting administrative practice within the British armed forces involves the reclassification of the military employee into a category other than 'Married'. The effect of this is that the employee becomes entitled to accommodation provided within barracks or Mess facilities, *and the licence to occupy the Service-owned Married Quarter is withdrawn.* This obviously has immensely important consequences on the marital partner remaining in the house. He (but much more commonly, she) is not the holder of the licence to occupy and therefore loses the right to remain in that accommodation. Instant eviction in the event of marriage breakdown is not the policy pursued by the British Services – indeed, a process of counselling and attempted reconciliation is obligatory before a decision to renounce the category 'Married' is accepted. Even after formal recognition that the marriage has collapsed, the administrative process requiring the married quarter to be vacated guarantees the occupying partner a period of at least three months before possible eviction is sought. In practice Irregular Occupants – the title bestowed within the British armed forces on people living in Service housing with no entitlement to do so – frequently continue their occupation much longer than the minimum guaranteed period of tenure.

However, the fact that military housing authorities may operate with a degree of benevolence in dealing with non-entitled occupants cannot disguise the housing risks likely to arise from divorce. In addition to losing the marriage and an adult partner, the individual left behind in the married quarter is exposed to potential homelessness. Within a few months, his or her rights to remain in the home will be extinguished. What happens thereafter depends entirely on the composition of the household – in particular, the existence of children – and the housing aspirations of the Irregular Occupants. If their wish is to be accommodated in social housing with some degree of public subsidy, then their future is highly uncertain, affected primarily by the demand for such housing in whichever part of the country they wish to settle in. The ability of public bodies to provide social housing has been decimated since 1980 as an act of deliberate central government policy intended to reduce the political importance and authority of elected local government agencies. Consequently, waiting lists for social housing have escalated, and entry to such housing has become far more uncertain, often also requiring lengthy waiting periods. As a result, families confronted with homelessness know that even if good quality social housing is eventually achieved, they face an interim period of unpredictable length consisting of dire, transient, inadequate temporary housing.

Not surprisingly, therefore, couples living in military housing have every incentive to stay together. More graphically, even a physically abused partner subjected to a regime of intermittent violence may fear even more the consequences of alerting welfare or other agencies which may end the terror at the price of losing the home. In this respect, partners in military marriages have fewer rights than their civilian counterparts, since divorce amongst civilians will not normally also imply homelessness for wives and children. What appear to be below-average marriage breakdown rates for certain years at least within the British Army and RAF may therefore simply reflect the high occupation rate of married quarters and the resulting necessity of remaining entitled to continue living in such housing whatever the degree of marital distress. As the table below illustrates, the Royal Navy displays divorce figures much more clearly in line with British average national rates. Notably, the Royal Navy is the only one of the British armed forces to have encouraged owner occupation amongst its employees and so, therefore, the threat of becoming homeless if the marriage disintegrates is far less acute.

Divorce Rates Per 1000 Marriages

	RN	Army	RAF	UK Average
1989				
Age				
16–24	28.7	10.2	11.8	25.4
25–29	31.0	18.9	16.9	31.1
30–34	26.5	20.4	13.7	26.1
35–44	15.0	15.9	10.5	18.5
45 & over	6.4	9.0	6.1	5.2

Divorce and the Armed Forces

	RN	Army	RAF	UK Average
1990				
Age				
16–24	32.0	10.8	12.4	23.1
25–29	35.0	20.7	15.4	31.0
30–34	29.5	20.8	13.4	26.3
35–44	19.2	18.9	8.7	18.6
45 & over	9.8	12.1	4.9	5.2

(Source: Personal Communication)

For entire populations – as opposed to military communities alone – certain age and social class groups are statistically more likely to divorce than the average, and although nobody is immune from the risk of divorce, irrespective of age or social group membership, approximately three-quarters of British divorces occur before the age of 50.

Proportion of all Divorces: by age group 1986

	Age 35	Age 40
Males	44%	66%
Females	54%	72%

By 1992, the median divorce age in Britain was 37.2 years (compared to a median age of 33.8 years in the USA), and 60% of United Kingdom divorces were occurring before one or both of the partners achieved the age of forty. This is particularly significant for military communities, since it means that the majority of divorces will occur during those years when men and women are in Services employment.

These figures comprise *all* divorces, not just those for first marriages. Within a marriage enjoying a potential length of over fifty years there are peaks and troughs of risk to the relationship. It is abundantly clear that the seeds of discord and ultimate divorce are often sown in the early years of the marriage. Thus

Thornes and Collard in their survey *Who Divorces* (*op. cit.*). found that over 50% of those eventually divorcing said that problems started within the first two years of the marriage. Similarly, the study of young marriage by Mansfield and Collard *The Beginning of the Rest of Your Life* (Macmillan, 1988) supported evidence that approximately one-third of British divorces occur by the fifth wedding anniversary. Communities which, in effect, encourage young marriages – as armed forces housing arrangements do – are therefore stimulating relationships amongst one of the most vulnerable age groups.

The younger the couple are at the date of marriage, the higher their risk of divorce. Thus, the marked reduction in the number of teenagers entering legal marriages in Britain shown in Chapter 2 should have a beneficial impact on future divorce rates. It is highly unlikely that Romeo and Juliet would have survived the course of a 50-year marriage. Early marriage has close links with social class and a pregnant bride, but dead-end jobs – or no employment prospects at all – are still likely to make the role of wife and mother attractive to young women. Persuading them to stay single longer therefore demands better work alternatives – a particular problem within military communities.

If divorce is analysed by the duration of marriage, it is abundantly clear that the earlier years engender the greatest stresses.

Proportion of Divorces by Duration of Marriage (Great Britain)

	Year of Divorce		
	1971	1981	1992
Length of Marriage			
0–4 years	13%	21%	23%
5–9 years	31%	29%	27%

(Source: Derived from OPCS data in
Social Trends Number 25, HMSO, 1995)

These figures suggest that an increasing proportion of British divorces occur before the tenth wedding anniversary.

Proportion of British Divorces Occurring by Year Ten

1971	44%
1981	50%
1992	50%

Although no marriage can ever be judged to be completely immune to the threat of divorce, the risk falls markedly after the ten-year stage.

Half of all British divorces do nevertheless occur to couples married for more than ten years, but this distribution is spread over a much longer time-scale.

In 1992, 31% of British divorces occurred to couples who had been married 10–19 years; 15% to couples married between 20–29 years; and 4% to couples married for 30 years or over.

There is no doubt that the early stages of a marriage appear crucial in its ultimate length. There is now abundant research on divorce in the United Kingdom which demonstrates that the genesis of an eventual divorce can be found in the first five years of a marriage. Although there are subsequent peaks in the number of divorce petitions filed – particularly around the twenty-year stage of marriage when children can be presumed to have left home and the couple are deprived of a mutual nurturing role – it is the balance of joy and misery in the early years of a couple relationship which seem to determine its outcome.

American divorce patterns are similar: by 1988, the average point at which divorce took place was after 7.1 years of marriage. The increasing proportion of divorces happening within the first two years of marriage shows up very clearly in the 1992 figures. It is counterbalanced by the fall in the number of divorces occurring in years 3–4. What this reflects are legal amendments to divorce law introduced into Britain as the outcome of the 1984

Matrimonial Proceedings Act, which permitted divorce after one year of marriage – previously, there had normally been a waiting period of three years.

Summary

This Chapter has reviewed the data on divorce and speculated on its causes, some of which are unique to military families, and others which are stresses experienced by civilians as well. There is little doubt that factors endogenous to military lifestyles – separation, frequency of geographical movement, difficulties in sustaining continuity in children's education and restricted spouse employment opportunities, for example – do impose strains on military relationships. In addition, military marriages are exposed to those exogenous hazards which imperil all contemporary marriages – the potential duration of any newly-formed marriage; altercations over role allocation and rule-making within the relationship; the outcome of the process of reflection about personal goals and the adequacy of the marriage conveniently summarised in the term 'mid-life crisis'; and the availability of alternative options to remaining within an unhappy or destructive marriage which allow for a greater application of personal choice in deciding to end such a relationship.

Legal changes have certainly facilitated divorce, but the causes of growing divorce rates lie within concepts of consumer sovereignty and the exercise of personal choice which have been imbued with largely uncritical approval in Western cultures. The notion of obsolescence has provided the same justification for replacing partners as for changing the television.

Some research evidence suggests that divorce occurs with greater frequency in military communities than amongst civilians. However, not all studies point indisputably in this direction. Despite the extra pressures to which military marriages are subjected, the majority survive. In part this may be because losing the entitlement to remain in military housing has extremely worrying consequences, and acts therefore as a brake on couples separating whatever their degree of marital misery. But in part also there are (or, at least, have been until the

1990s) considerable benefits from membership of military communities – reliable and reasonably well-paid employment, assistance with housing, education and social welfare needs – which have enabled Service personnel to weather the storms of marriage discord. Probably, divorce patterns within the military largely reflect those happening in the surrounding civilian society. Certainly some of the old barriers to divorce within the armed forces have been removed – divorce no longer leads to dismissal or the requirement to resign, for example – and the obligation introduced by equal opportunities legislation for military institutions to accept single parents as *bona fide* employees, sharing with differently structured households the same equal rights to promotion, means that such individuals – often divorced – cannot be stigmatised or automatically rejected as suitable candidates for advancement. Those military employees with high career ambitions no longer have to be (and remain) married in order to achieve them.

CHAPTER 5

The Rise and Rise of the Professional Woman

War is man's work. Biological convergence on the battlefield would not only be dissatisfying in terms of what women could do, but it would be an enormous psychological distraction for the male who wants to think that he's fighting for that woman somewhere behind, not up there in the same foxhole with him. It tramples the male ego. When you get right down to it, you've got to protect the manliness of war.

(General Robert Barrow, former Commandant of the US
Marines, from 'The Marine Corps Faces the Future',
New York Times Magazine, 1980)

There have, of course, been a number of charismatic female military leaders – Boudica, Joan of Arc – as well as the legendary Amazons of Dahomey to refute claims that battle has always been exclusively a male preserve. Nevertheless, female warriors have always been regarded as eccentric abnormalities, an atypical response to particular social and military circumstances. Fighting has been predominantly a male activity, indeed characterising the gender, and the term 'woman combatant' still seems contradictory to many people, both male and female. A number of women disguised as men have successfully entered the armed forces in the past. The most famous British example is probably Dr James

Barry, who served with the Army Medical Department for over 40 years, retiring in 1859 with the rank of Inspector General. Only after her death was Dr Barry's gender discovered.

Developments since 1980 – both in weapons technology and in demographic change – have, however, led to substantial increases in the proportion of Servicewomen within the armed forces of Western industrialised countries. In 1987 NATO produced the following information about female membership of its forces:

Women in NATO Armed Forces 1987

Country	No. of Women	Women as % Total
Belgium	3,496	3.8%
Canada	7,724	9.1%
Denmark	821	3.0%
France	20,470	3.7%
West Germany	141	0.03%
Greece	1,640	1.0%
Italy	None	0%
Netherlands	1,644	1.5%
Norway	540	1.4%
Portugal	9	0.001%
Spain	None	0%
Turkey	No data	No data
United Kingdom	16,323	5.1%
United States	220,250	10.2%

In 1995 the Committee on Women in the NATO Forces provided further evidence on the attitudes of member states to the employment of Servicewomen.

Belgium: Women are fully integrated into the armed forces and amount to 6% of all military personnel.

Canada: 11% of regular forces are female. There are no restrictions on postings except to submarines.

Denmark: Women are fully integrated into all three Services. They have been employed in combat roles since 1988 and were cleared for fighter pilot training in 1993.

France: Women employed in all three Services, theoretically in all roles, including combat roles.

Germany: Roles still extremely restricted for women; limited to unarmed medical personnel and musicians only.

Greece: Other than nurses, the employment of women is still relatively uncommon and regarded as experimental.

Italy: Uniquely within NATO, Italy still has no female members of its armed forces. Change has been discussed but as yet no action has been taken.

Netherlands: There are no restrictions placed on employment roles for women in the Dutch armed forces. The numbers have increased substantially since 1987 and are expected to reach 8% of total personnel strength by 1996.

Norway: Norway demonstrably practises a policy of total sex equality. There are no restrictions on the roles women can undertake, and they are employed in every role from infantry to tank commanders; they also serve in submarines.

Portugal: The first female entrant (a doctor) was accepted in 1989. Progress has so far been cautious.

Spain: In 1988 all armed forces branches were opened to women, but in practice restrictions remain and the numbers employed are still small.

Turkey: There has been a substantial increase in the number of women employed in unarmed supporting roles. Since 1993 entry to officer grades has been opened to women in all specialties except infantry and armour.

United Kingdom: Separate female Services have been abolished and women completely integrated into the armed forces. In practice, restrictions still apply to certain combat roles: specifically in infantry, tanks and submarines. The first British female *Tornado* pilot qualified in 1995.

United States: Women represent some 11% of all US military personnel. In theory they enjoy equal opportunities, but in practice remain excluded from combat roles in armour and infantry. By 1995, America had seven female pilots of attack helicopters.

As this information indicates, not only have the numbers of women employed as members of armed forces increased, so too have the roles they undertake within those Services. It is these role changes which induce the anxiety and consternation expressed by General Barrow contemplating the growing involvement of women within the US Marine Corps. How can a man do what a man's got to do if a woman is alongside equally capable of doing it? Where is the quintessence of masculinity if the exclusive right of men to engage in combat is destroyed? And surely battlefield leaders must be male if they are to generate the loyalty and magnetism necessary for Servicemen to put their own lives at risk?

> Men are taught to have a stake in the military's essence – combat; it is supposedly a validation of their own male 'essence'. This is matched by the military's own institutional investment in being represented as society's bastion of male identity. That mutuality of interest between men and military is a resource that few other institutions enjoy, even in a thoroughly patriarchal society.
> This mutuality of interest has the effect of double-locking the door for women. Women – because they are *women*, not because they are nurses, wives or clerical workers – cannot qualify for entrance into the inner sanctum, combat. Furthermore to *allow* women entrance into that essential core of the military would throw into confusion *all* men's certainty about their male identity and thus about their claim to privilege in the social order.
>
> (Cynthia Enloe, *Does Khaki Become You?*
> London: Pandora, 1988; p. 15)

Servicewomen represent a recruitment response to particular economic, demographic and technological circumstances. But their steadily growing involvement in a wider and wider range of military occupations challenges orthodox assumptions about capabilities and gender roles. It is what women are now doing in the Services – and what they may do in future – which provokes controversy and doubt amongst Servicemen.

WOMEN IN THE SERVICES

Women have long been associated with armies, though only relatively recently have they been accorded the status of being on the paid strength. 'Camp followers' is a description of great longevity, and would be understood in many previous centuries to refer to the motley crowd – predominantly female – who followed soldiers on their campaigns. The roles were mixed: washerwomen, wives, prostitutes and nurses, with one individual sometimes combining some or all of these functions. But no European army marched without its train of camp followers. Typically, in the seventeenth century an army of 40,000 men would be accompanied by 100,000 followers – a substantial tail to teeth ratio.

The Crimean War (1853–56) provoked much discussion about the relationship of women to the British Army, and some substantive changes. The ministration of Florence Nightingale and her colleagues converted nursing wounded soldiers into a respectable and worthy activity for middle-class ladies. The same stubborn, indomitable spirit which led Octavia Hill to establish low cost, sanitary social housing for the poor, or Mary Carpenter to campaign tirelessly for separate institutions for juvenile offenders, enabled Army nurses – with the important help of the media – to expose the gross incompetence which characterised the prevailing levels of medical care. Florence Nightingale brought into the Crimean hospitals administrative and logistical skills of a superior order, making an irrefutable case not only for best-practice nursing skills but also for women to manage this area of the military world. A British Army Nursing Service was established in 1881, with women occupying the key roles.

The 30 years after the Crimean War also saw a prolonged debate about the merits of soldiers marrying. As no accommodation or other support was offered, this was in practice difficult for all but the most senior, so that in 1871 only 1.5% of British soldiers aged 20–24 were married, compared with 23% of the civilian population. Effectively, wives were discouraged as excess baggage which could hamper the deployment readiness of their husbands.

Services nursing developed into specialist provision through the Queen Alexandra's Royal Army Nursing Corps (QARANC) and comparable organisations for the Royal Navy and the

RAF. These nursing services were both exclusively female and *ancillary* to the organisations of uniformed, fighting men.

Servicewomen were an invention of the First World War in Britain. The Women's Army Auxiliary Corps – later the Queen Mary's Army Auxiliary Corps (QMAAC) – was formed in 1916 to provide women for service in France. Its formation was due entirely to a manpower shortage. The QMAAC members worked as drivers, storewomen, telephonists, clerks, cooks and waitresses, so releasing men for the frontline – a doubtful benefit. For the first time, women were in Army uniform, and paid military salaries.

The QMAAC was disbanded in 1919, but the precedent of using women in wartime had been established. In 1938 the Auxiliary Territorial Service (ATS) was created, and by 1943 215,000 women were serving in it. Over one hundred different trades were opened to women, and they were paid two-thirds of the equivalent rate for men. (*The Soldiers: An Anatomy of the British Army*, Henry Stanhope; London: Hamish Hamilton, 1979, p. 242.)

A small contingent of ATS members was kept in existence after the Second World War, and in 1949 this was subsumed, along with the QARANC, into the newly created Women's Royal Army Corps (WRAC). For over 40 years, the WRAC provided a separate set of careers for Servicewomen as part of the British Army until segregation ceased in 1993 with the incorporation of women into the Army as soldiers and officers. Separate women's Services in the British Navy and Royal Air Force were also brought to an end, their members being re-established as mainstream members of their Service at the same time.

Recruitment to the separate women's Services in Britain fluctuated according to the availability of suitable males. Enlistment targets for Servicewomen were perceived as a variable factor which could be adjusted up or down according to the state of the employment market. Work roles assigned to women were supportive rather than combatant, though the range of tasks undertaken gradually widened. Significantly, women were not taught how to use small arms (or other weapons) until the 1980s, although women members of other NATO armed forces did receive weapon training. When the WRAC did introduce this for its members in 1981, it was specifically for 'self-defence', so seeking to maintain the essential supportive rather than combatant status that a capability to use weapons might imply.

Debates of much longer standing had derived from questions of appropriate dress. Should QMAAC members have breast pockets on their tunics? Would ordnance officers object to issuing underclothes to the ATS? What degree of femininity should be permitted, or even demanded, of Servicewomen – in particular, what cosmetics could be accepted and how should hair be worn?

> Ambivalence about the meaning of women-as-soldiers continues to plague military uniform and cosmetic designers. A woman in the present day American Army is instructed to keep her hair short enough so that it just reaches the collar of her uniform but *not* so short that it looks 'unfeminine'.
>
> (Cynthia Enloe, *Ibid.*, p. 119)

Retaining a clearly defined female identity has been, and remains, symbolically important. It is helpful to the contemporary NCO that the mouth under the helmet and above the flak jacket is wearing lipstick as it permits easy recognition within a mixed-gender platoon on exercise. Disputes about what Servicewomen should wear symbolise the enormous significance of clothing as a gauge of permitted tasks and social functions. It is not surprising, therefore, that arguments over clothing have been much more extensive than debate on the merits or drawbacks of Servicewomen learning to handle weapons. The ending of segregated women's Services in Britain has not led to an identity of uniform with their male counterparts: Servicewomen are still expected to be visibly feminine and to wear a range of clothing which distinguishes them as female members of the armed forces.

WHY DO WOMEN ENTER MILITARY SOCIETIES?

Military organisations are the archetypal patriarchal social systems. Can Servicewomen therefore expect to maximise their career potential within such structures? Is to become a female member of the armed forces a statement of heroic intent to undermine those traditional patriarchal values, to strike a blow for the women's movement? Or does it reflect the more mundane realities of economic disadvantage experienced by women, an opportunity for employment with some possibilities of career enhancement and an escape from what may be more limited or non-existent civilian employment options?

American feminists have conducted an anguished debate as to whether a woman can join the military with any serious expectation of modifying such a sexist organisation from within. Their conclusion is that the task is impossible, and that 'liberated' women already serving in the armed forces wish to avoid hearing this message as it denies the legitimacy of their attempts at reform. (see Enloe, *op. cit.*). However, the assumption that women join up for ideological, rather than economic or social, reasons seems improbable.

The US *Defense Manpower Data Center* reported the following information on *African-American Women as Percentage of Active Duty Female Officers and Enlisted Personnel* between 1971–89.

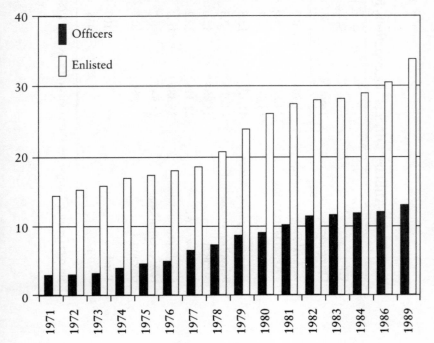

Military Officers' Occupations by Gender and Race/Ethnicity (%)

Military Occupation:	Total N	Black		Hispanic		White	
		W	M	W	M	W	M
General/Flag Executive	1,705	0.0	0.2	0.0	0.2	0.1	0.7
Tactical Operations	124,511	4.9	35.1	8.0	36.8	7.8	46.8
Intelligence	13,694	4.1	3.5	4.8	4.3	6.4	4.4
Engineering/maintenance	41,101	13.8	19.4	11.0	16.0	10.4	13.4
Scientific/professional	13,305	2.3	3.6	2.7	3.6	3.9	4.6
Medical	43,894	35.6	8.1	40.0	12.6	42.8	11.1
Administrative	22,316	22.2	10.7	20.7	7.9	17.9	5.7
Supply/procurement	25,380	16.0	15.3	11.9	9.7	8.7	7.7
Non-occupational	14,941	0.7	3.9	0.9	8.7	1.6	5.4
Unknown	564	0.2	0.2	0.0	0.1	0.2	0.2
Total %		100	100	100	100	100	100
N		4,458	16,437	729	5,289	27,316	238,625

Source: Defense Manpower Data Center, December 1989.

As black women are about 11% of all US women, they are slightly over-represented in the officer corps and three times more likely to be found in enlisted grades than their population proportion would predict. Analysis of the roles carried out by women in the US Services reveals over half to be employed in either the 'Medical' or 'Administrative' categories, but in this black women are no different from white.

> The rapid increase in military enlistment of minority women is large-ly attributable to such factors as a decline in the number of men in the 17–21 age cohort, high rates of unemployed black and Hispanic youths as well as lengthy political struggles for equality of opportu-nities, which has helped to influence expanded opportunities in the military.
>
> ('African-American Women in the US Military', Brenda L. Moore, *Journal of Armed Forces and Society*, Spring 1991)

Because women – whether black or white – have been largely recruited to 'support' rather than 'teeth arms' occupations, they are disproportionately vulnerable to post-Cold War personnel reductions where the intentions are to protect and maintain high quality combatant capability from predatory accountants.

Redundancy could be especially disruptive to those women who joined the armed forces as a calculated, if interim, career move. Junior ranks, in contrast to officers, frequently enlisted to escape from what they perceived as a boring existence in back-water communities: the Services offered new avenues and opportunities, and women were particularly likely to use the continuing education facilities to obtain qualifications or seek entry into higher education. Female officers, who had often already a substantial history of educational achievements behind them, were more likely to express anger over their exclu-sion from command in many military appointments because of the female combat exclusion rule.

However, two recent developments in Europe may provide some defence for women against disproportionately large per-sonnel cutbacks – the greater participation of women within the armed forces in a widening variety of military occupations, including many from which women had previously been excluded; and the extension of European Union equal opportunities policies to the armed forces of member states, which has proved particularly dramatic and costly to the United Kingdom.

WOMEN AND COMBAT

That women should not directly participate in combat featuring members of armed forces made considerable sense when such conflict involved hand-to-hand fighting, the use of heavy broadswords and axes, wearing armour and, to bring us up to date, any strenuous exertion involving upper body strength. Despite the fact that much heavy manual labour – particularly in agriculture – is carried out by women throughout the world, their comparative lack of physical strength has always been advanced as a reason why women should not participate in that special kind of manual labour called combat.

However, it is abundantly clear that in contemporary nondomestic conflicts a simplistic distinction between 'combatant' and 'non-combatant' roles can no longer be drawn. Modern warfare means that targets are frequently appreciably distant, visible only through the medium of imaging equipment or radar. The controls which launch weapons at unseen enemies are electronic, requiring not enormous physical strength but only the touch of a series of buttons. Patently there is no reason why women need exclusion from such work on the grounds of insufficient physical strength. That they continue to be debarred from 'combat' roles owes much more to social convention and the unwillingness of men to recognise that women could competently perform such activities.

> . . . the military's sexual division of labour is rooted ultimately in two rather tenuous notions: first that there is a clear line between 'combat' and 'non-combat', and that second there is a geographically real place called 'the rear'. If 'the front' is not where combat exclusively occurs, there is no way to ensure the survival of the essential masculinity of the military as an institution and the gendered basis of militarist ideas which legitimise it.
>
> (Cynthia Enloe, *op. cit.*, p. 153)

At present, it is by no means certain that all Servicewomen *want* the entitlement to take part in 'combat' roles in any case. Indeed, there is some evidence that non-officers are equally divided on this issue. Female officers, on the other hand, resent their exclusion from (male-defined) 'combat' activities because this is precisely why their command opportunities – and therefore their ultimate military career achievements – are so limited. Senior Servicewomen who comprise the Committee on Women in the NATO Forces share this ambivalence, but state that whilst women may not *choose* to take up combat roles, they must be able to exercise such a choice free from discriminatory laws. (Reported in *The Guardian*, 22 February 1995). Defining specified tasks as 'combat' or 'combat-related' conveniently guarantees that men only need apply, and that there will be no female competition.

In 1985 the French Parliament ruled that women were eligible for all armed forces branches, including those previously designated as 'combat' and therefore male. The only areas to which this policy was not to apply were the French Foreign Legion, commando units, and fighter aviation.

This last exemption seems little justified, and the British RAF, for example, has female fast-jet pilots. Excluding women from command and operational participation in units traditionally still requiring hyper physical fitness and extreme bodily strength – marine, commando and paratroop specialisms are obvious examples – has more rational justification.

In France, however, the 1985 decree produced little speculation about the equal opportunities implications of the measure. Instead, much debate was provoked as to whether this meant that women, as well as men, should now be conscripted to fulfil national military service obligations, and, if so, for how long. Certainly, genuinely equal treatment of women within the French armed services logically demands a review of the conscription issue. In practice, the French Defence Ministry does not see such an exemption as incompatible with equal treatment for women within the Services, arguing emotively but without customary Gallic logic that women constitute the sex giving life and men the sex taking life. If this is to be the foundation for gender policy within the military, then it would be more rational to maintain a 'combat role' exclusion zone for women rather than use it to avoid conscripting females.

What these changes within the French armed forces have brought about is discussion – and some research – on the consequences for leadership within the French military of greater sex equality. Military leadership as a distinct process has been exhaustively examined and debated by historians and by educators within armed forces training establishments. 'Leadership potential' is the greatest virtue ambitious Services personnel need to demonstrate if their careers are to advance. Yet such qualities are difficult to analyse and isolate, nor is it clear that leadership within military settings is uniquely different from management within a school, a hospital or a boardroom.

However, military leadership has been almost solely identified with men, particularly where it has been perceived as deriving from charismatic qualities within individuals which have invested them with an aura of moral authority. Is this an essential feature of successful military leadership? If so, could women offer this style of leadership? Would soldiers be willing to die for female commanders?

Jean Boulegue of the University of Paris has examined the attitudes of male French Air Force conscripts to women NCOs since the opening-up of occupations within the armed forces to women. He hypothesised that whereas men would accept female leadership based on demonstrated technical competence and superior knowledge (leadership based on what Weber termed 'rational legitimacy'), it was unlikely that women leaders would be regarded as charismatic personalities evoking fierce emotional loyalty and attachment.

Boulegue's research was carried out in the mid-1980s, but reported as 'Feminization and the French Military' in *The Journal of Armed Forces and Society*, Spring 1991. The male conscripts were under the control of female physical fitness and drill instructors. Attitude surveys undertaken amongst these recruits established, as expected, that professional competence shown by the female NCOs was respected. What was unexpected was that some NCOs aroused 'considerable ardour' amongst conscripts, who were particularly keen to win approval from these instructors. In discussion with the researchers and other conscripts, these instructors were vehemently defended with a loyalty which went far beyond simple acknowledgement of professional competence. So perhaps female military commanders can demonstrate charismatic leadership qualities, inspiring devotion and valour from their troops.

Of course, this French research took place within the limited confines of basic training: it was not a battlefield situation. Because of 'combat role' exclusion policies, little investigation of how Servicewomen perform in conflict scenarios has been possible. However, Charles Moskos in *Female GIs in the Field* reported on Servicewomen deployed in a major US Army exercise in Honduras in 1984. Most of the soldiers (men and women) were located at Palmerola airfield, a military base in Central Honduras, but an aviation battalion was also deployed in the jungle close to the El Salvador border.

Enlisted women soldiers were performing duties such as communication specialists, drivers, doctors and nurses and clerical service staff. The female officers were mainly doctors or helicopter pilots. The bases from which the military exercises were launched were subject both to dust storms and heavy rain. The heat was oppressive, the humidity high. Only two rooms were air-conditioned: the operating theatre in the field hospital and a video games room. Accommodation was in wooden huts. Males and female were segregated. Latrines and showers were outdoors, screened and sexually separate.

These conditions were relatively luxurious compared to the up-country aviation battalion, which was accommodated in tents. The policy in the field was for work sections to sleep in the same tents: if women were in a section with men, they shared that tent too. Blankets hung from internal tent ropes offered some spatial seclusion, but aural privacy was non-existent and some women complained of the vulgar language of their male tent-mates. Women using the field latrines and showers were guarded by female colleagues. Moskos observed that the experience of sharing such primitive living facilities brought about behavioural changes for both sexes.

The men generally displayed increasing awareness of female sensibilities – if not to the degree that the women would have preferred, at least enough to allow for the emergence of a *modus vivendi*. On their part, the women's concern for personal privacy quickly eroded over the course of the field experience. Within a week or so the prevailing female attitude developed into one of 'let 'em look'. It became too much trouble for the women to try to maintain conventional standards of privacy.

(C Moskos, 'Female GIs in the Field', *The Journal of Armed Forces and Society*, Autumn 1985)

Interestingly, female officers in this Honduras exercise were less concerned about privacy and decorum than female soldiers. Moskos suggests that this:

indicated the greater reluctance of women officers to acknowledge any male/female differences. Admission of such differentiation could easily be used by the military to rationalise a reversal of the trend towards full incorporation of women into the armed forces. Inasmuch as the enlisted women generally saw their stay in the military as being for a single term, the long-term implications of acknowledging male/female differences were less consequential.

Advanced pregnancy would, of course, exclude women from full participation in military roles, but in this respect employment in the armed forces is no different from working in the civilian labour force where countries with maternity benefit systems require temporary withdrawal from employment for the welfare of both mother and unborn child. But would menstruation reduce the effectiveness of Servicewomen? This issue has been rigorously analysed for the American Defense Department. The absence and sickness rates of Servicewomen have been compared to their male counterparts to assess the impact of menstruation and pregnancy on fitness-for-work rates. The evidence suggests that in fact military males lose proportionately more time available for active duty than females, mainly because of drug- and alcohol-related misdemeanours, going absent without leave and discipline-related offences.

Certainly Servicewomen do not exhibit higher sickness or absenteeism rates than males, and arguably they represent often a better rate of return on the resources invested in their professional training. The opposite view – that Servicewomen have a higher attrition rate than men because they leave voluntarily on marriage or at childbirth – may become a less defensible proposition once wider career options within the armed forces are recognised by women as genuinely and permanently available. In addition, wastage rate amongst female recruits has been officially recognised within the United States as linked with sexual harassment. The Department of Defense has ordered commanders to prevent sexual harassment, in part as a retention strategy. Such an edict is likely to have limited effect until or unless the promotion chances of senior military personnel are linked to the numbers of Servicewomen who drop out.

EQUAL OPPORTUNITIES

Between 1978–95 the British Services compulsorily dismissed approximately 5,000 Servicewomen because of pregnancy, normally five months before they expected to give birth to their children. These actions were taken by the Ministry of Defence confident in the legality of its exemption from the 1978 European Community's Equal Treatment Directive.

However the European Court of Justice subsequently ruled this armed forces opt-out to be a contravention of European Union social policy, which had superior jurisdiction. From 1991, the Ministry of Defence accepted that their actions were subject to the Equal Treatment Directive, and sought to offer compensation payments of five months' salary to dismissed Servicewomen – this representing employment lost between the date of dismissal and the subsequent birth of a child.

However, Industrial Tribunals – to whom ex-Servicewomen appealed against discharge – rejected this approach and awarded more substantial amounts of compensation. In 1994, in a sex-equality case unrelated to the military, the European Court of Justice removed the relatively low ceiling (£11,000) that had limited compensation for compulsory discharge. As a result, claims flooded into the MoD from women now seeking financial recompense not only for income lost to date *but for future anticipated earnings as well.* In the case of female officers – who could anticipate serving until the age of 55 – this might represent between 20 to 30 years of salary. In one highly publicised case – a Royal Navy nursing officer made pregnant by a Roman Catholic Chaplain – compensation of £350,000 ($500,000) was paid. In December 1994, a former Army Captain sought damages of over £500,000 for loss of future earnings, calculated on the basis of probable career length. However, the Ministry of Defence appealed successfully against the amount, which was reduced to £25,000 ($40,000). This represents only some 5% of the original claim, and this case is clearly being used as a precedent by the MoD to reduce subsequent compensation payments. Nevertheless, informal calculations suggest that ultimately the Ministry stands to lose some £40m in compensation payments for illegal dismissals, as well as incurring a less easily quantifiable additional cost, that of recruiting and training women for professional military roles.

Although it is the monetary claims of former British Servicewomen who were required to resign because of pregnancy which have received considerable publicity, it is in some ways other aspects of equal opportunities legislation which may in the long term be even more significant. In a rather bizarre manner, the Ministry of Defence succeeded in antagonising the Industrial Tribunal system on another, but related, issue in February 1995. This was the refusal of the MoD to reveal to the Tribunal documents relating to its policy on sex discrimination. The Tribunal was considering a claim for compensation from a Servicewoman dismissed for pregnancy, and ordered the disclosure of official papers which formed the basis of Ministry decisions. MoD lawyers have, so far successfully, challenged the right of an Industrial Tribunal to see such documents, and have indicated that the Ministry would in any case seek a Public Interest Immunity Certificate – a gagging order – if it lost its appeal against the order to disclose such material to the Industrial Tribunal. The MoD is effectively attempting to argue that its policies on sex discrimination and pregnancy dismissal constitute official secrets, which it is against the public interest to reveal.

The essence of equal opportunities policies is that sex discrimination is outlawed both as to employment conditions and salaries but also in terms of maintaining rules and procedures designed to prevent access by women to particular occupations. Employers retain the right to select staff on the basis of perceived and relevant merit, but not to operate guidelines designed to exclude particular genders, or racial groups, as a matter of routine. The 'combat role' exclusion rule is obviously vulnerable to challenge in terms of sex discrimination. It has little contemporary justification whatever its historical rationale may have been, but the outcome of such a rule has the crucial effect of denying women entry into the top echelons of the British and American armed forces. Exclusionary policies are *prima facie* in breach of equal opportunities legislation. An appeal to the European Court by a determined British Servicewoman refused promotion to a post because of her gender will eventually succeed.

Of course, many women may blanch at the prospect of achieving total equality within the military through acquiring unequivocally the right to kill. Ironically this poses a feminist dilemma, whether the establishment of such equality is worth the price paid – the adoption by women of policies designed to lead to the mutilation and death of human beings identified as enemies. It is precisely this capacity for aggression and violence which has been identified by many feminists as uniquely and lamentably male. In order to establish their entitlement to be absolutely equal, need women also demonstrate a capacity to be equally lethal?

In some respects, the military already offers women a wider range of occupational choice and achievement than does civilian life. Juanita Firestone found that:

> although the military as a whole is extremely male intensive, the proportionate distribution of women and men in the military, across occupational categories, is more representative than the distribution of women and men across civilian occupational categories.
> (Juanita Firestone, 'Occupational Segregation Comparing the Civilian and Military Work Force', in *The Journal of Armed Forces and Society*, Spring 1992)

The major difference in the range of occupations undertaken by women in this survey was the higher proportion of them in engineering and technical specialisations within the US armed forces compared with the numbers of women engaged in similar high status employments in the civilian labour force.

The British armed forces have adopted formally the positions of 'equal opportunity' employers. In a similar fashion to America, women within the British Services occupy a wide range of posts and exceed the proportion of women in skilled engineering, electrical and electronic careers within the UK. Women sailors now go to sea, airwomen service and fly aircraft, and women are integrated into British Army units. Undeniably the range of opportunities open to Servicewomen has been dramatically extended, and probably exceeds those available to civilians. It may in consequence seem churlish to cavil at what has been achieved by women within the armed forces. Yet until women regularly obtain some at least of the most senior appointments possible within the military world, the suspicion must remain that what has transpired, although more than mere tokenism, represents less than wholehearted commitment to the cause of equality.

In the United States, the armed forces have adopted a trenchant approach to equal opportunity issues. The US Air Force, for example, issued the following *Action Memorandum* on 'Command Responsibility for Equal Opportunity' in February 1994:

In today's quality Air Force, the contribution of each member becomes increasingly important. Accordingly we must ensure that all of our people are given the opportunity to reach their full potential. Air Force policy on equal opportunity is straightforward: military members and civilian employees will be provided equal opportunities and treatment regardless of age, color, national origin, race, religion, sex, or, in the case of civilian employees, disabling conditions.

Summary

The insistence of military authorities that women be prevented from undertaking certain types of tasks on the grounds that they constitute 'combat roles' has diminishing logic about it. In practice, such a policy conveniently excludes females from competing with male colleagues to occupy prestigious positions within the armed forces, and denies them entry to the uppermost career echelons as a result. Challenges by Servicewomen using equal opportunities legislation look increasingly likely to succeed once it is recognised that banning women from combat has little to do with contemporary warfare but a great deal to do with protecting the careers of senior male Service personnel by reducing the competition.

CHAPTER 6

Farewell to Loyal Campfollowers?

OFFERING COMFORT AND SUPPORT . . .

Wives accompanied members of the British Indian Army overseas in the nineteenth century, but in other British and all American armed forces, no arrangements were made for wives and children until after the First World War. Social roles for wives, except for the Commanding Officer's wife, were not prescribed by military culture until much later, and then the approved behaviour was largely a similar but subordinate version of the roles defined for the CO's lady.

Once the military population began to extend beyond serving personnel to encompass wives and other family members, so concerns about this community and its welfare began to emerge. The CO's lady in the British Indian Army was expected to concern herself with the welfare – moral and practical – of other wives, principally through providing social occasions such as dinners, dances and attendance at sporting events featuring the husbands.

In the second half of the twentieth century, community integration and development tasks were undertaken to a significant extent by certain wives in the British Army, and to a much lesser extent in the RAF. Welcoming newcomers, inducting them into the Service community and organising assistance during times of family pressure – because of illness, for example, or during and after the birth of a child – became significant roles attaching to the wives of specific males within the Army hierarchy.

As well as the Commanding Officer's wife, the wife of an Officer Commanding (OC) a sub-unit, and the wives of senior NCOs acquired the status of key figures within the community, and crucial participants in the induction process for new members. However, no payment was ever made for wives who adopted these roles, and no training provided. Minimal Service resources were made available to support this essentially voluntary process – rooms in which community activities could occur (later replaced by Community Centres) and minor expenditure on printing to inform people of community activities. Wives Clubs and community Coffee Mornings became the sanctioned vehicles for achieving some of the desired social objectives.

Women married to Navy personnel were far less exposed to these pressures. Naval wives never served with their husbands on board ship and were able to choose a geographic location in which to buy or rent housing, remain static and enter into the local civilian labour market, with children attending local non-Service schools. Naval families have typically been integrated into civilian communities to a much greater extent than their Army and RAF counterparts, and consequently the wives of Navy husbands have perceived their commitments as being to their families and to their own careers rather than to the Navy.

The higher degree of accompanied mobility experienced by Army and Air Force families has therefore imposed certain expectations on specific wives to play leading parts in facilitating the reconstruction and stabilising of communities constantly exposed to turbulence (house moves) and ever changing social membership. Within British military culture the wives of key unit personnel have effectively been invested with the critical roles of community organiser and comforter of the newly arrived. Unchallenged assumptions that such wives were available, suitable and willing to undertake these tasks prevailed until the 1970s.

SUSTAINING SOCIAL CONVENTIONS

From the viewpoint of the chain of command the roles undertaken by senior wives represented an extremely valuable and cost-effective resource. True, there were minor costs in providing accommodation and related services, but in return their integrative activities induced not only a sense of well-being and a caring community but also the promotion of a particular pattern of social behaviour designed to sustain the structures and social conventions judged apposite for military lifestyles.

New arrivals were offered not only essential local information on coping and surviving in the new setting, but also a range of approved leisure pursuits in which participation was encouraged. Identified events, such as Christmas Dinners or an annual unit dance, would be attributed a high degree of importance, and an appropriate code of dress would be sanctioned. Attendance of wives, and where appropriate of children too, whilst it could not be ordered was nevertheless expected by the chain of command. Non-appearance would require convincing explanations, since compulsory socialising on certain occasions was perceived as a unique way of fostering a sense of group identity and belonging. It also required people to recognise *where* they belonged – in a Service setting where the demands of the employer overrode familial or personal ambitions.

The welcoming, induction and absorption of new community members are undoubtedly valuable tasks. They represent an acknowledgement of the threats to personal and family stability resulting from change, offer assistance in identifying the gains to be achieved from the move, and above all signal that the receiving community wishes to hold out the hand of friendship. The importance of these tasks for the well-being of Service community members cannot be exaggerated, and they remain pressing and continuing requirements even with fewer accompanied overseas deployments.

However, should these activities be left to volunteer wives? Is it only wives of specified Service personnel of particular rank who should in any case have this involvement? To what extent was there any genuine 'volunteering'? And did the assumptions on which such a system was based continue to apply – that suitable wives were available to carry out these community develop- ment tasks? And what evidence was there that the goal of social integration sought by the military system was in fact being achieved?

Such questions were being asked with increasing persis- tence in the British armed forces from the mid-1970s onwards. This was a period when each of the Services con- ducted searching reviews about its own welfare needs and shortcomings. One of the conclusions to emerge was that whilst systems for creating a sense of belonging and commu- nity identity remained vital, the presumption that this could safely be left to active volunteering from wives was queried. Changes within military communities had made it far less likely that traditional self-support integration schemes would automatically flow from, for example, Wives Clubs. One of the principal reasons for this was the increasing proportion of Service wives in paid employment.

DUAL CAREERS IN MILITARY FAMILIES

The proportion of Service wives in paid employment has con- sistently been below that of civilian married women. This is especially so for wives accompanying serving husbands overseas and away from their home country. In these circumstances, employment prospects have always been more limited, some- times by the local terms of agreement under which the military base is sanctioned but often by language barriers.

Moreover, the age structure of military communities features women at their peak reproductive stage. Unless there is kin support or available and affordable childcare facilities, young mothers appear less prominently in the labour force, even amongst civilians. Since mobile Service wives experience a deficit in kin support, it is to be expected that their employment participation rate would be lower than overall UK or American average figures.

However, military communities have reflected the increasing percentage of married women who engage in paid employ- ment, even if at a somewhat lower level.

Economic Activity of British Women with Dependent Children in 1994

Age of Child	Working Full-time	Working Part-time	Unemployed	Economically Inactive
0–4	16	30	6	48
5–10	20	45	6	29
11–15	34	40	4	22

The table above provides information about women working in the civilian labour force in Great Britain. It measures the extent of involvement in paid employment, and clearly shows the effect of dependent children on the ability of women to participate in the labour force. For all women who are living in households with or without children under the age of 16, the proportion economically active is as follows:

Working Full-time	Working Part-time	Unemployed	Economically Inactive
36%	29%	5%	30%

Female employment patterns in America demonstrate similar trends.

Women in the US Labour Force: Participation Rates

	Single	Married
1970	57%	41%
1980	64%	50%
1993	66%	59%

The most recent data on the employment of Service wives come from the *Wives Continuous Attitude Survey (November*

1993 – March 1994), by S J E Smith and A Hampson. This consists of responses from a random sample of 1,500 Army wives, and is reported twice annually. Asked: 'What is your employment situation now?' produced the following information:

In full-time employment	23.3%
In part-time employment	28.3%
In self-employment	2.5%
Seeking employment	17.5%
Not seeking employment	26.9%
In full-time education	1.2%
In part-time education	2.1%

Although proportionately fewer Army wives are in work than their civilian counterparts, the ratios are not that dissimilar if it is borne in mind that the military community has a younger age profile and the number of Service wives with either no children or children who are no longer dependent is relatively small. But a significantly larger percentage of Army wives is in the category 'seeking employment' – 17.5% – compared with the civilian unemployment rate of 4%. Many of the wives rated their job prospects as bad and were frustrated at the difficulties of maintaining their own careers. A typical comment was: 'The greatest problem has been the difficulty of my job prospects. I am a highly qualified and experienced Nursing Sister but had to take more junior posts each time we moved until eventually I was unable to get a post at all.'

In 1993 Sally Moran – herself a nurse married to an Army husband – produced a research report on *Dependant Nurses in a Hidden Community* for the Federation of Army Wives. Moran studied the effects of a geographically mobile lifestyle on the employment experience and qualifications of nurses who were also Army wives, and compared their employment pattern with a cohort of civilian nurses. Among the difficulties identified for military wives who are also nurses were:

• difficulties for Enrolled nurses in securing conversion courses to become Registered General nurses;

- access to midwifery updating training; and
- gaining promotion above basic employment grades.

Moran found 75% of Army wife-nurses to possess higher level nursing qualifications – a proportion substantially in excess of the UK national nursing average. Compared with civilian nurses, double the number of Army respondents reported taking career breaks. One-third of Army wife-nurses have been unable to work professionally because they were overseas and security considerations or local language barriers were obstacles, and 42% said they had experienced times when no suitable work was available. Opportunities for professional development were far more limited than for civilian nurses, and this had important long-term career implications.

Where the Army itself employs wives, its policies on pay and conditions were often seen as exploitative: 'The women who are in full-time employment, such as myself, work long hours for the Army and get paid so little. We should get paid a lot better for the amount of work we do.'

As the employment figures quoted earlier shows, older married women with children in school, or whose children have grown up, have a higher participation rate in the UK labour forces. But it is precisely this group who have constituted those senior wives expected to offer voluntary community support services. A clash of interests has developed between military systems seeking continuous, but free, integration and induction practices, and the career ambitions of the wives themselves.

Such conflict is not, of course, unique to military societies. The collision of personal career ambitions entertained by spouses with the demands of their partners' employer is a recognised feature of business and diplomatic communities too. Soraya Tremayne makes the following observations about 'Shell Wives':

> The point of compromise between expected conformity and tolerated independence in wives must, of course, shift over time. Non-conformity is a fact for management, more now than even a decade ago . . . The younger generation of Shell wives, particularly

Farewell to Loyal Campfollowers?

the relatively career-minded and highly educated, are the least tolerant. While they thought they had chosen a man as an equal and as a partner for life, they now find themselves in a segregated and very unequal position in which any control that *is* possible is exercised by him. They resent being vetted by the company before going on a posting. They are unwilling to give up a career for which they may have spent many years training in favour of their husbands'. If they do so, however, they expect to retain some personal autonomy rather than become totally absorbed within their husbands' professional identity.

('Shell Wives', by Soraya Tremayne in *The Incorporated Wife*, by H Callan and S Ardener (eds); Croom Helm, 1984)

In the United Kingdom the increasing proportion of the labour force constituted by women has produced conflicting political and social comment. Whilst feminists commend paid employment as the primary goal for women seeking to maximise individual potential, opposite opinions express regret that such a development is at the expense of children receiving adequate parental care. Anxiety about what is happening to and within families has produced much-trumpeted fears that family structures are imminently disappearing, and that in part such changes result from the greater economic independence women have acquired through higher labour force participation.

British governmental policy has been driven by a Treasury naturally disposed to reducing public expenditure and able to exploit the moral ambiguities and uncertainties about the merits of advancing women's employment in order to resist substantial publicly funded childcare programmes. As a result, although pre-school provision has featured on the political agenda since proposals for its dramatic enlargement were presented by the then Secretary of State for Education Margaret Thatcher in 1972, no significant progress in public funding for educating children under five has been made. However, in July 1995 the Education Secretary Gillian Shepherd announced a new initiative. On a pilot basis in limited areas in 1996, and on a nationwide basis in 1997, vouchers would be available for all children aged four. Parents would be able to buy pre-school provision for each four year old, topping up the £110 value of each voucher where nursery fees were higher. It remains to be seen whether this development leads to an expansion of educational experience for the under fives. Clearly, it does nothing for children aged three, and may simply recycle the cost from parents to government where four year olds are already benefiting from pre-school provision. The advantages deriving from the American *Headstart* affirmative action programme for disadvantaged children is widely acknowledged across the British political spectrum, but the 1995 British initiative does not target inner-city or lower-income children specifically.

Although the extent of proper public funding in pre-school education remains unresolved, there has nevertheless been considerable expansion in privately funded pre-school programmes. But these are not universally available throughout the country and, of course, present a cash barrier to poor households. In consequence, Britain has lagged behind other European Union member countries in the provision of pre-school opportunities.

Percentage of Children with Publicly Funded Childcare Places 1985/6

	0–2 years	3–5 years
Belgium	23	95
France	23	95
Italy	5	88
Denmark	44	87
Spain	5	66
Greece	3	62
Germany	3	60
Ireland	1	52
Netherlands	2	50
Luxembourg	1	48
UK	2	44
Portugal	4	25

(P Moss, *Childcare and Equality of Opportunity*, Report to the European Commission, 1988)

Moral uncertainties about the merits of married women working – especially young mothers – has also characterised attitudes
within the British armed forces. Pre-school provision has been
commended in a series of Service studies examining military
communities and their needs (Seebohm 1974, Spencer 1975,
Finch 1978, Wood 1977, Gaffney 1987, etc.). However, the
focus has always been on providing opportunities for children
to learn and mix together socially rather than freeing mothers
for employment. The Playgroup movement has been whole-
heartedly welcomed by British military authorities and formal
links established with the influential Preschool Learning (formerly Playgroup) Association, which has provided advisers and
training for Service community members setting up playgroups.

However, enabling Service spouses to obtain paid employment has not been seen as a legitimate role for the UK armed
forces. Such assistance as does exist for married partners to find
employment has come from voluntary self-help movements
within Service communities.

In the forefront has been the Federation of Army Wives
(established in 1983 as the Federation of Army Wives Clubs)
which has set up a database of skills held by participating member wives which is made available to local employers. Similarly,
employers who file details about their labour needs are matched
with appropriate database members. However, this system is
not available throughout the UK, so that British Army wives
experience differing degrees of support in their search for paid
employment.

In contrast to this minimalist approach to supporting spouse
employment ambitions, the American Army Spouse
Employment Program is an established and publicly funded
system enabling marriage partners to obtain work. Its justification has been the belief that spouse satisfaction has a positive
influence on retention rates within the US Army. An analysis of
this system by Schwartz and his colleagues (*Journal of Armed
Forces and Society*, Vol 17, No. 3, Spring 1991) revealed that:

• older, more experienced spouses were more likely to be in the
  labour force,

- Army spouses with children under five were less likely to be employed,
- spouses located near population centres had better job prospects than those in the relatively isolated Army locations typical of many deployments,
- spouses with higher educational levels and updated job skills were more likely to be employed,
- the length of time Army households are stationed at a particular location is statistically significant in spouse work rates,
- employment prospects were worst for spouses located outside the United States, either because of work restrictions on US citizens or because of job scarcities.

The authors of this study concluded that providing spouse employment programmes, lengthening the time families are based at particular places and supporting training programmes which increase the education and job skills of spouses all had positive influences on spouse employment rates. Above all, the US Army was perceived by spouses as a positive, supportive employer, a factor identified as highly important in re-enlistment or retention decisions.

BEING A SUPPORTIVE WIFE

The employment patterns revealed in this American study are very similar to those applying to British military communities too. Particularly when located in the United Kingdom, older rather than younger spouses are more likely to be in employment, and in remote, rural stations work prospects for partners are severely limited. That the British armed forces have not followed the US Army approach to spouse employment is partly a funding issue, but there have also been greater ideological objections.

Firstly, employed spouses – especially wives – by definition will be less available to continue the tradition of voluntary welfare support within the Service community. And secondly, where spouses pursue their own careers, rather than simply take temporary jobs, they are far more resistant to accompanying the Service member on posting to a new location.

One of the contributory factors increasing resistance to regular house moves was the pressure in the UK during the 1980s to buy a personal house and become an owner-occupier whilst still in the Services. Encouraged by a range of government financial inducements, owner-occupation expanded rapidly in Britain during this period so that by 1992 69% of all UK households either owned outright or were in the process of buying their homes. Whilst Navy families reflected this trend very closely, far fewer Army families became owner-occupiers. Thus only 37.5% of wives responding to the 1994 *Wives Continuous Attitude Survey* were owners. However, the expansion of owner-occupation during the 1980s was achieved largely by transforming existing tenancies into ownership arrangements. This meant an important change in the legal relationship between the people concerned and their houses, but it did nothing in itself to increase available accommodation. One effect it did have was to reduce substantially the quantity of 'social housing' – rented accommodation provided in the main by local authorities (public community bodies in American terms). Because Service personnel had looked historically to such social housing for their future occupation when they left the armed forces, the reduction in the availability of this kind of housing obliged them to consider house purchase earlier than they might otherwise have done. And having acquired ownership status – and expensive mortgages to accompany it – there were often considerable pressures in such households for wives and children to stay behind when the Serviceman was posted yet again.

This combination of housing and employment factors produced the phenomenon of so-called 'voluntary unaccompanied service' in which spouses stayed behind, frequently in their own homes, continued with their personal careers, and often provided daily care for children who were able to attend local civilian schools. In contrast, the Service member ceased to reside with the rest of the family, and was accommodated in communal facilities offering little privacy but much opportunity to drink.

Such marriages are put at considerable risk, and as the underlying cause is seen as being the desire for spouses to maintain their own careers, no official assistance has been provided to help partners find employment (except at the Service member's duty station) since the practice undermines the desired social structure, that married Service personnel will be accompanied by their families except when engaged in deployments which specifically make that impossible.

Being a supportive wife involved more than mere physical presence. Accompanying a Service husband was recognised as contributing significantly to his morale, and therefore his professional military performance. Beyond that, however, by being in the same location the Serviceman's wife was also making a commitment to the Service, and an acknowledgement that the demands of the Service constituted the number one household priority.

Why, however, should such wives engage in voluntary community support behaviour?

In part, this reflected a genuine sense of mutual responsibility for the members of the military community, who shared common lifestyles which tended to segregate them from civilian society. Isolated rural locations, frequent house moves, periods of enforced separation, these all were features in the social experience of Service wives which distinguished them from their civilian counterparts. These shared lifestyles which differentiated them from civilians forged a sense of common identity and a sympathetic awareness of mutual pressures and problems. Faced with the periodic absence of husbands, it was scarcely surprising that military wives created support systems within the community from which they would themselves benefit from time to time. Thus, the development of social integration and support systems through voluntary actions from wives was not simply a 'top down' pressure from the chain of command. The creation of a friendly, welcoming society capable of offering informal assistance at times of family pressure was advantageous to everyone.

In addition to the practical value of living in a helping community, altruistic instincts also played a part in the involvement of many of its members in common activities. A recognition, particularly by older and more life-hardened community members, that newcomers were exposed to severe family and personal stresses encouraged these senior members of military societies to maintain and develop helping mechanisms.

Whilst the wives of senior British personnel did not attend community development training courses, the wives of designated Commanders in the US Air Force did participate in orientation training on acting as a CO's wife. Senior wives from both countries in practice found themselves heading-up informal family support systems designed to provide a set of interactive networks intended to forestall isolation and generate rapidly a sense of common identity and purpose. When the system worked well, it replicated precisely the same kind of manoeuvres carried out by paid community workers in British 'New Towns' and in inner-city areas on both sides of the Atlantic.

However, it would be wrong to conclude that this pattern of social assistance was entirely voluntary. Beneath the spirit of altruism and the undeniable mutual benefits lurked also the anxiety that failure to participate would damage the careers of Service husbands. The 1987 American Air Force Blue Ribbon Panel Report on *Spouse Issues* demonstrated that many wives did not believe the official USAF policy, which reiterated the right of spouses to find paid employment if they wished to, and considered instead that to make career progress in the Air Force meant accepting the unwritten 'two for one' policy – a policy which expects wives, especially senior wives, to forgo employment opportunities and career aspirations in order to participate fully in Air Force life. Significantly: 'Almost all spouses, regardless of the member's rank, expressed displeasure with the "two for one" concept, and feared that the system would be slow to change; they felt that field commanders set policy – not the Pentagon.' (USAF, *Spouse Issues* Report; Pentagon, 1987)

This American study revealed major differences of view over the entitlement of the Service to expect compulsory altruistic activities from military spouses. The wives of senior officers, especially commanding officers, remained generally favourable to a system to which they contributed substantial unpaid personal resources of time and energy, but from which they derived meaningful status within the community. Many younger wives, in contrast, resented this informal network which, in their view, was primarily gratifying the needs of senior wives and did not provide a support system which they themselves would be willing to use. Nor did they wish to have to engage in such Air Force approved activities themselves, although they recognised the risks to their partners' careers if they refused to do so. The *Spouse Issues* Report concluded:

> 'The majority of wives are supportive of their husbands' careers. They do, however, resent the apparent dual standard in the system; it is all right for the husband of a military woman to work in the civilian community, but if the wife of a military man works, she is often perceived *as shirking her responsibilities to the Air Force family*.' [Author's italics]

As a direct response to this Report, the US Air Force issued a revised *Air Force Instruction* on 'Members' Marital Status and Activity' (AFI 36-3010; April 1994) This advised: 'This instruction prohibits commanders, supervisors, or other Air Force officials, from using the marital status of the member, positively or negatively, to affect the career of the military member. This prohibition pertains to performance evaluations, promotion, assignment, or command opportunities.' This is a strong restatement of previously existing policy. However, in view of the belief expressed by many respondents to the *Spouse Issues* study, that it is in reality local commanders who create effective policy towards spouses, it is obviously unlikely that a central decree of this kind will be perceived as categorical evidence of the abandonment of the 'two for one' system.

There are many parallels between the debate within the American Air Force and the arguments which have raged within the British Army. On occasions, for example, sections of the British Army have insisted that the role of Commanding Officer or Regimental Sergeant Major (the unit's 'supreme soldier') could only be filled by personnel who were married and accompanied by their wives. Not only must such wives subsume their own careers, they must also act as the twin pillars of the community support system.

Such expectations have not been the experience of British Army wives only. The wives of industrial executives have also been expected to engage in conformist behaviour, supportive of their husbands. *Fortune* magazine long ago issued the following instructions to wives in an article by W H Whyte on 'The Wives of Management' specifying that they should be:

> 1. Highly adaptable. 2. Highly gregarious. 3. Realise her husband belongs to the corporation. A good wife is good by not doing things, by not complaining, by not being fussy, by not engaging in controversial activities.
>
> (*Fortune*, October/November, 1951)

Nancy Shea's *The Army Wife* for over 25 years provided a handbook for the wives of American soldiers covering military customs, rank courtesy and etiquette. It was made very clear where a husband's loyalties would lie: 'Early in your new role as an Army wife you must understand that your husband's "duty" will come *first* – before you, before your children, before his parents, and before his personal desires and ambitions.' Moreover, various social obligations were detailed: 'It is every wife's duty not only to join, but to take an active interest in the wives' club on the post where her husband is stationed.' (*The Army Wife*, Nancy Shea/Anna Perle Smith; Harper & Row, 1941–66.)

In theory, of course, the employer – the Army – has no direct interest in or control over the spouse of one of its employees. Records are not kept exclusively about wives. How, therefore, would it be known whether or not a woman had demonstrated sufficiently appropriate and supportive behaviour for her husband to become CO or RSM?

In Britain the answer lies in the system of annual confidential reports which form the basis of promotion decisions. Although these reports do not include sections inviting specific references to spouses, in practice comments about marital partners do occur. Phrases indicating that Major/Sergeant Promotee has a history of being accompanied and ably supported by his wife are not uncommon. To the experienced reader, this is coded information which could be influential in final decisions. Moreover the absence of such a statement about the spouse can also be interpreted that the candidate for promotion does not bring with him the desired social support system. Readers of confidential reports become adept at analysing what is missing as well as what is included.

The British Ministry of Defence denies that evaluations of spouses feature in confidential reports. Whilst strictly accurate, this is also disingenuous. Comments about marriage partners are not actually prohibited, and in any case, it is the widespread belief within military communities that spouses are reported on which encourages social conformity and the sacrificing of personal career goals to those of the Service partner. It is the perception of what occurs, rather than the reality, which controls behaviour. Such a perception is convenient to the chain of command, and all members of Service communities understand that this is so. Official refutation of the idea that wives are appraised in confidential reports is simply disbelieved.

In 1994 the *Wives Continuous Attitude Survey* (the second in a series of studies being undertaken by the Director of Personnel (Army) and carried out by the Army Personnel Research Establishment) was distributed to a sample of 1,467 British Army wives. One of the questions asked was: 'I feel that the Army takes the wife's behaviour into account when considering her husband's career.' 24.3% of those who responded 'Strongly Agreed' with this statement and a further 42.2% 'Agreed'. Only 15.4% of those who answered disagreed. Invited in the same survey to comment on the somewhat ambiguous phrase: 'I feel that the Army expects me to behave in a certain manner.' 81.5% either agreed or strongly agreed.

NO LONGER A DEPENDANT

While anxieties about promotion prospects of the Service partner and the recognition that these may well be enhanced by engaging in 'voluntary' community support activities remain strong pressures on military spouses, other social and economic developments have tended to produce shifts in the opposite direction.

Apart from the pressures to enter into paid employment, other social changes have also tended to undermine the idyll of the mutually supportive, interactive Service community. Key factors here have been the rise in educational standards amongst spouses and a decreasing willingness on the part of wives to accept the status of 'dependant'.

Formal educational attainments have risen steadily in the United Kingdom since 1970. Output-measures of the school system which affect military communities include in particular the proportion of school-leavers who are qualified to enter university by virtue of achieving specified grades at *Advanced* level (and the Scottish equivalent) in the British national *General Certificate of Education* system.

Percentage of School-Leavers with Two or More A-Levels

	1970	1990
Girls	13%	22%
Boys	15%	20%

At the other end of the educational spectrum, the numbers of young people ending formal schooling with *no* educational qualifications has moved in the opposite direction. Only 7% of girls left without any recognised qualification in 1990 (compared with 12% in 1980). For boys, the comparable figures were 10% in 1990 compared with 15% a decade earlier. (Data derived from *Department for Education* statistics)

The British armed forces recruitment pattern reflects these advances in educational attainments, and spouses of Service personnel do as well. Contemporary data about the educational background and attainments of British Army wives demonstrate this. In answer to the question What Qualifications Do You Have?:

University Degree	6.5%
Higher Education Diploma	10.8%

A Levels or equivalent 20.2%
GCSE or equivalent 67.9%
Professional qualification 23.9%
No formal qualifications 16.6%
(*Wives Continuous Attitude Survey*, 1994)

Army wives parallel in many respects the enhanced educational achievements of women in British society over the last 20 years. The A Level scores are very similar, and the GCSE figure slightly exceeds the 64% of the civilian population obtaining at least one GCSE pass at any grade in 1989–90. However, there is a higher proportion of wives in Army communities who have no paper qualifications compared with their civilian peers.

Highly educated people are in general more self-reliant, and a clash has ensued between them and the Service community culture which they identified as benevolent but paternalistic and controlling.

An uneasy awareness that the British armed forces were failing to address such social change – and indeed, were perhaps guilty of seeking to ignore its consequences – led to a study reviewing the experiences and attitudes of British Army wives carried out by Colonel Mike and Mrs Jenny Gaffney (*The Army Wives Study: Part One*, 1986; *Part Two – The Way Ahead*, 1987.) *The Army Wives Study* had wide-ranging terms of reference: to determine those aspects of Army life which cause problems and aggravation for wives, and to recommend changes. The study authors spoke to 2,000 British Army wives worldwide. What emerged were some expected causes of concern – the frequency of moves; separations from husbands; variable quality in Army housing; anxieties about children's education; and difficulties in maintaining careers.

The Gaffney Reports made a number of recommendations to improve the life-quality of Army wives. More stability in Army postings, enhanced welfare support systems and an increased entitlement to move personal possessions at public expense when husbands were deployed overseas dealt with some of the major issues raised by wives.

However, the main thrust of these Reports, and their historic significance, lies in their recognition of the urgent and paramount need for attitudinal changes on the part of the Army itself. What was expressed over and over again to the Gaffneys was the sense of loss of identity by women who married soldiers. Overnight they ceased to be adults in their own right – and with their own rights – and became instead a 'dependant', with highly truncated rights compared to civilian wives.

Married women were reduced to 'wife of', or 'W/O', and a woman receiving treatment or giving birth in a British Military Hospital was identified on the bedhead and in her medical notes as 'W/O 12345678 (this being her husband's Army number). Overseas, Army wives could not borrow books from military libraries without first obtaining a signature from their husbands enabling them to acquire membership cards. Above all, housing was allocated exclusively to the husband. His wife had no entitlement to housing in her own name, and if the husband abandoned his wife in an Army house, she would rapidly cease to have any right to stay there. Army wives thus faced not only the extinction of their own personal identities as adults, but were also aware that they were exposed to far greater housing insecurity than civilians. In obtaining repairs to Army housing, wives frequently felt belittled by the housing management system: 'Wives become sensitive to real and imagined discourtesy and see in their treatment by low level officialdom an open expression of what wives often feel is the Army's true estimate of their worth.' (Section 8.2, *The Army Wives Study: Part One*).

Even where Army culture was perceived as benevolent, it remained paternalistic. And it was not always considered benevolent anyway. In any event such traditional attitudes were identified by *The Army Wives Study* as at best inappropriate and at worst offensive to the great majority of Army wives. The overwhelming message from this study was that higher educational attainments, greater career expectations and personal ambitions characterised modern women marrying soldiers, and that a social system perhaps appropriate for their grandmothers demanded urgent reconstruction if retention rates were not to be adversely affected by discontented wives.

That the British Army still has a long way to go in acknowledging wives as full adult members of the community is revealed by the *Wives Continuous Attitude Survey* (*op. cit.*). One of the questions designed to measure attitudinal change was: 'I feel that the Army regards me as a person in my own right.' The response to this was overwhelmingly negative:

Strongly Agree/ Agree	Neither Agree nor Disagree	Strongly Disagree/ Disagree
6.7%	18.7%	74.6%

The WCAS study comments that 'perceived attitudes to wives' was the most frequently cited issue throughout the survey. Some of the comments wives made included:

. . . many of the wives feel they are treated as second class citizens by the Army. There don't seem to be any rewards for being patient, supportive and a one-parent family for months, sometimes years on end . . . I do feel that wives are not treated as equals. They are not given due respect and most of the time are treated as half wits who don't know any better.

and another wife said:-

Being ex-Army myself I noticed a great change with the Army personnel's attitude towards me. I found I was expected to possess absolutely no common sense, little intelligence and was expected to rely on my husband for everything, which as far as I was concerned couldn't be further from the truth. I have always been a very independent person and really do resent being classed as an extension of my husband.

An utter determination to reject dependant status had caused one wife to leave Germany and return to the UK:

The appalling manner in which I have been treated by the Army has led me to leave my husband in Germany and assume a civilian lifestyle on my own with my children. The depersonalisation I experienced was overwhelming. The expectations made of me because I am my husband's wife were outrageous. The rules to which I was subjected can only be described as archaic and pathetic.

Although the British Army featured in this particular research exercise, the lessons learned applied to a lesser extent to the RAF too, where Servicemen were expected to be accompanied by their wives wherever located. However, the Air Force had less of a paternalistic tradition than the Army, subjected its families to a lower frequency of moving and provided better quality housing. Nevertheless, women with their own careers and a determination to maintain their own independence still found themselves exposed to Service expectations of supporting their husbands. That the demands to do this were less openly expressed made for situations of ambiguous uncertainty for RAF wives. These difficulties have been excellently described by Ruth Jolly in *Military Man, Family Man: Crown Property?* (London: Brasseys 1987).

Summary

Women marrying Servicemen enter a society significantly different from that of civilian wives. The cultural systems constructed to offer integration and support for such wives had also the objective of prescribing approved behaviour. Employment and educational changes have rendered such social systems increasingly irrelevant or offensive to contemporary women, but vestiges of past paternalism still remain. Moreover wives still remain concerned that their own individual lifestyle might prejudice their husbands' careers, despite official denials that wives are part of the assessment process. In addition, military communities are only beginning to come to terms with the growing number of partners who are men married to Servicewomen.

CHAPTER 7

Sex: the DS Solution

WRAC Sergeant June Osborne and her husband Corporal Andy Osborne were serving in the British Army in Germany. Their best friends were another couple also both in the Army – WRAC Corporal Maureen Lawrence and her husband Corporal John Lawrence. Both couples were in their early twenties, had been married for two years and there were no children. All of them worked within the same large military garrison area.

One Saturday morning the Army Families Office was informed by Cpl. John Lawrence that his wife was missing – and also that Cpl. Andy Osborne was absent too. Neither had returned home after completing their late working shift the previous day.

On Sunday evening Maureen Lawrence and Andy Osborne appeared in camp, but refused to go to their respective married quarters. They announced they were in love, wished to divorce their present partners and marry each other. Cpl. Andy Osborne also said that posting Maureen Lawrence and himself to separate Army locations would bring neither of them back to their current partners, that he and Maureen were determined to marry and would spend every minute of leave together, and that, in any case, it was none of the Army's business if they fell in love and married.

In all military decision-making, there is always a DS (Directing Staff) solution: a correct answer to a problem. This is just as true in areas of human sexuality and personal relationships as in dealing with technical or logistical concerns. Specified types of sexual activity are approved and pass the DS orthodoxy test. Other patterns of sexual behaviour are condemned or discouraged, and severe sanctions are applied to non-conformists ranging from rebuke to dismissal.

Servicemen have always exploited their power, affluence and physical distance from home to engage in sexual indulgence, and this remains true in the contemporary British and American armed forces. Yet the predominant norm remains that of heterosexuality within legal marriage, and assistance in the form of subsidised housing and Family Welfare agencies have been used to promote the desired structure. Promiscuity by unmarried Servicemen has not been perceived as conduct requiring military control, and such behaviour has a long pedigree in Britain. The preamble to the English Act for Relief of the Poor (1601) identified among the groups which constituted especially troublesome malingerers: 'lewd wandering mariners and licentious soldiery who expose their wounds and seek alms'.

Unmarried Servicewomen, on the other hand, have historically been exposed to much greater institutional interference in the formation of personal relationships on the assumption that young women need such protection. When separate women's Corps existed within the British armed forces, considerable supervisory resources were committed to their defence against the anticipated sexual stratagems of Servicemen. Even today the prospect of single Service personnel living away from base – perhaps with a cohabitee rather than a legal spouse – still rouses heated emotions for some military commanders. Imminent changes in the provision of Services housing through the Defence Housing Executive, however, will consign apoplexy over such matters to history. Not only will single parents who are military employees occupy married quarters, there will also be opportunities for unmarried members of the Services to obtain military housing too. The political imperative to utilise military housing and lower the non-occupancy rate will supersede any questions about the propriety of who lives in particular houses. In future, the chain of command will exercise a much more restricted degree of control over such matters.

So if Corporal Andy Osborne and Sergeant Maureen Lawrence do go ahead with their respective divorces and marry each other, a military house will be available to them. Precisely *where* that accommodation will be, however, is not within their control. And it is still highly likely that the chain of command will not willingly accept this change of marital partners simply as a *fait accompli*. To do so would be to undermine the official DS policy of encouraging married heterosexuality within life-long monogamous partnerships. Unless Osborne and Lawrence are punished in some way, their declared future plans represent a successful challenge not only to the partners in their existing marriages but also to the preferred model of marriage itself.

As all British Army and RAF families know, the standard response to affairs and sexual liaisons is physical separation of the couple involved. Often, new postings are found for both parties and computerised records ensure that co-location will never occur in the future either. Of course, such control is weaker when one member of the defaulting couple is a civilian – a Service spouse, for example:

British Army Corporal Alec Hathaway (35) has been married to Anne (34) for 12 years. They have two sons aged ten and eight. They are currently located in Germany.

For the past three months Anne has been having an affair with Staff Sergeant Graham Armstrong. Armstrong is married but unaccompanied by his wife in his present posting. He is living in the Sergeants Mess where Anne Hathaway works as a waitress. The relationship between Anne and Graham became possible because Alec has been away from home for five months out of the last six on training and promotion courses.

Alec Hathaway came to suspect something was wrong when he returned during a mid-course leave period. Anne confessed to the affair, but claimed she now wished it to end and that she proposed to return to her mother's house with the boys for a few weeks to allow tempers to cool and to sort out her feelings. Cpl. Hathaway has reported the affair to the Major commanding his unit. He says he still loves his wife, and will accept her back but wants the Army to take action against the predatory Staff Sergeant.

In this Hathaway could rely on the Army taking prompt, punitive action, as he was well aware. Staff Sergeant Armstrong was marched in front of the unit's Commanding Officer, censured as to his conduct and relocated in a large depot area in the UK. Apart from his difficulties in explaining to his wife why he was suddenly returning to the UK, Armstrong was in effect fined heavily – since he would lose what at that time were valuable Overseas Allowances for serving in Germany – and any ambitions he might savour of joining the officer class (being Commissioned) also disappeared at a stroke.

The entitlement of Service authorities to intervene in personal relationships derives from military law. The justification is the belief that operational effectiveness demands dependable teamwork, which in turn rests on shared trust and respect. Such trust and respect will be undermined if members of the Services – officers and senior NCOs in particular – exhibit flawed personal lives. Publicly demonstrated standards of excellence in probity and personal morality are required, for without such demonstrated characteristics respect will not be retained. Leadership within military systems stipulates that superior standards of moral behaviour in comparison to civilian norms are necessary – in alcohol consumption, the use of non-legal drugs, and the management of personal finances behaviour must be exemplary. But, above all, unbecoming conduct is most threatening to order and discipline when it relates to sexual peccadilloes.

The British armed forces have periodically reminded their members about expected standards of personal behaviour. Most recently the Army in its *Discipline and Standards* paper (MoD 1993) repeated this advice. In his introduction to this document the Adjutant General outlined the Army's reasons for issuing guidance on matters of personal behaviour and the responses which disapproved conduct would produce. He argued that the purposes of *The Discipline and Standards Paper* were purely functional.

The strict code of conduct required in the Army is not the continuance of outdated Victorian moral standards or a desire to set an example for society. We operate within a close-knit community where teamwork, cohesion and trust are paramount. Those who undermine this position by their behaviour are failing in their duty to the Service. While it is not possible to list all forms of behaviour that would have this effect, broad examples are given. The message is clear: that which is illegal or undermines operational efficiency is not tolerated.

The Discipline and Standards Paper was widely distributed. All Commanding Officers were required to discuss personally issues which it raised with fellow officers and senior NCOs, and it was required that it should feature in all promotion and post-basic training courses.

The paper begins by regretting that

> . . . in more recent times . . . a divergence between the standards expected in the Service and what many take as acceptable within civilian society has led to an increasing questioning and lack of understanding of the reasons for the military's strict code of conduct.

> Within society the formative influences in promoting positive attitudes towards authority have been in steady decline: religion, education and the family no longer always provide the framework of behaviour, social structure and responsibility they have in the past. More liberal attitudes prevail, leading many parts of society to reject or reduce in importance those values which the Armed Forces seek to maintain and regard so highly: sense of duty, loyalty, self-discipline, self-sacrifice, respect and concern for others.

The paramount need for superior conduct is then spelled out. High standards of discipline are essential elements in professional military competence, the foundation on which motivation, morale and leadership are based.

> The operational imperative of the Army stresses the importance of the group over self-interest. Armed conflict is, by its very nature, a

group rather than an individual endeavour. A sense of unity, cohesion and loyalty are decisive factors in any armed conflict. Nothing must be allowed to detract from the forging of close bonds, based upon mutual trust and respect, between members of the group, and between the group and its leaders.

It follows from this that: 'The behaviour of those in positions of authority must be exemplary, otherwise their usefulness, effectiveness and proper relationship with all ranks will be impaired.'

Specifically in what the *Discipline and Conduct* paper terms 'social misconduct' unacceptable heterosexual relationships are listed. Adultery 'is likely to prejudice the position of an individual and may bring the Army into disrepute.' The location and outcome of adulterous relationships are also relevant matters:

Adultery within the Military Community
The most serious cases of social misconduct involve adultery within the military community. It is essential that military personnel are not worried about the integrity of their marriages at any time, but especially when deployed away from their home base.

Adultery outside the Military Community
Married or single officers who enter into adulterous affairs *outside* the military community jeopardise their status as an officer should the circumstances of the affair become public, and if it brings the officer or the Army into disrepute.

The Army also spells out the problematic nature of sexual relationships between a couple who are both Service members:

The Army is based on a clearly defined hierarchical structure, with distinctions between the different ranks that are well-understood and accepted, as is the particular division between officers and non-commissioned ranks. *Sexual relationships which undermine this well-ordered structure cannot be tolerated.* (emphasis added)

While there would be no objection to a consensual liaison

between a junior non-commissioned officer and a private of opposite sex, the same would not be true of a similar liaison between an
officer and a non-commissioned rank. Such relationships diminish
the authority and standing of the superior in the eyes of his subordinate resulting in a loss of credibility and trust.

While marriage between an officer and a non-commissioned
rank is not prohibited, such relationships will inevitably cause difficulties, as the couple will not be permitted to serve in the same
unit.

The 1994 case in which a female British Army Captain married
to a Lieutenant Colonel was fined £1,200 for her affair with a
junior-ranked soldier illustrates the system's determination to
prevent liaisons which cross the rank divide. Because the
woman involved chose to publicise the way her personal life was
being determined by the Army authorities – by declaring her
story to the tabloid press – she was subsequently court-mar-
tialled as her conduct (in talking to the newspapers) was judged
to have brought the Army into disrepute.

The idea that the behaviour of staff can damage corporate
reputations and induce 'disrepute' is one that has had lengthy
currency amongst established professions such as medicine, law
and the church. Doctors, clergymen and lawyers are required to
subscribe to codes of conduct, breaches of which are well understood to mar or ruin careers. Such codes have been introduced
to protect the interests of patients or clients against the less
scrupulous practitioners. They are a necessary protection for
customers engaging self-employed professionals.

That the British Army punishes specified conduct on the
grounds that it may bring the image of the entire organisation
into 'disrepute' indicates a continuing attempt to equate Army
service with the accepted professions such as law and medicine.
In reality, individual Army members are not self-employed professionals but rather constituents of a very large structure with
clear command chains and lines of management to which they
have immediate responsibility. If personal behaviour prejudices
their competence in performance, it is line managers who
should respond appropriately. Poor time-keeping, indiscipline,

failure to achieve agreed work targets are all proper subjects for the concern of an employee's chain of command. An extra-marital liaison in itself need have no impact on work performance, to which there is abundant testimony throughout politics, business and public services in both Britain and America.

Employers do not normally seek to dismiss staff who have affairs, though they may sometimes be moved to other sections of an organisation in an attempt – usually unsuccessful – to reduce gossip. Personal relationships are not viewed as a legitimate area of interest for the employer, nor is the concept of 'disrepute' and commercial damage to the organisation seen as a likely outcome of consensual affairs between staff members. By maintaining, through Queens Regulations, the right to discharge employees who have been judged by senior members of the armed forces to have brought 'disrepute' to a particular Service, the military system is seeking to impose on Service personnel what are perceived to be the admirable and desired higher moral standards of self-employed professionals.

Guidance about acceptable conduct existed when Staff Sergeant Armstrong became involved with Corporal Hathaway's wife. His banishment and disgrace were therefore known risks. Unfortunately for him, and the Army, the threat of subsequent punishment is unlikely to constitute much of a deterrent to individuals swept up in the excitement of grand passion.

SEXUAL HARASSMENT

Because of a concern that sexual harassment was leading to a costly wastage rate amongst Servicewomen, the US Department of Defense issued orders to Commanding Officers in 1981 to eliminate such conduct. Such edicts from the DoD against sexual harassment may not only effect some change in male behaviour, they also, in elevating the issue to the point at which national policy guidelines are produced, succeed in raising awareness that sexual harassment constitutes a form of social transgression, rather than simply a personal problem. Once defined as a societal problem, support and rescue avenues must be made available to victims. Moreover, publicity must be attached both to the unacceptable nature of the behaviour and also to the remedies which can be sought. Identifying sexual harassment as behaviour not to be tolerated within military communities would be expected, therefore, to increase the number of complaints.

In practice, Servicewomen appear to have varying personal definitions of what constitutes sexual harassment and the extent to which reporting incidents to superiors would be either appropriate or useful. In his study 'Female GIs in the Field' (*The Journal of Armed Forces and Society*, Autumn 1985) Charles Moskos detected differences between female soldiers and officers in the American Army on this topic. He comments that although many of the enlisted soldiers had experienced some form of sexual harassment, it did not seem to be a major concern to them. '. . . the women maintained that a firm "No" would usually be sufficient. [They] believed it was up to the woman herself to handle incidents of sexual harassment: recourse to a superior – almost always a male – was considered a last and probably ineffectual resort.'

Female officers, on the other hand, were much less tolerant of sexual harassment. In part this may have been because they interpreted the term more widely. Whereas female soldiers defined sexual harassment mainly in terms of sexual propositions, officers were inclined to extend the term to mean any practices which they perceived as discriminating against women, including the definition of what constituted suitable military work for women and the combat exclusion rule. Such an understanding of the term is no doubt wider than that intended by the Pentagon, and offers a further line of challenge to present limitations on the permitted roles of women within the armed forces.

One form of harassment which was mentioned to Moskos by female soldiers was propositioning from lesbians. The true incidence of lesbianism – or for that matter male homosexuality – within the US Services is unknown, but: '. . . accounts of lesbians were offered spontaneously in most extended interviews with female soldiers. The general impression was that lesbianism caused much less alarm among women than did homosexuality among the male soldiers. Male soldiers would express disdain, if not threats of violence, against homosexuals; the women were more likely to espouse an attitude of live and let live.'

The British Army *Discipline and Standards Paper* also refers to sexual harassment in the following way:

> Sexual harassment is unacceptable behaviour. There can be no simple definition of sexual harassment but it may be described as unwelcome conduct of a sexual nature, or other conduct based on sex, which degrades the dignity of an individual of the opposite sex. Sexual harassment can be persistent unwanted attention which continues after the recipient makes it clear that he or she wants it to stop. A single incident, however, can also constitute sexual harassment if sufficiently serious. Sexual harassment is not a criminal offence in itself, though certain forms of sexual harassment can result in criminal charges: for example, indecent assault.

This definition has the merit of recognising that both men and women can be victims of sexual harassment. On the other hand it identifies it as conduct purely of a heterosexual nature. By doing so, it ignores one of the anxieties often raised about homosexual behaviour within the armed forces – that it provides a charter for bullies.

HOMOSEXUALITY

Homosexuality, male or female, is incompatible with military service because of the close physical conditions in which soldiers often have to live and work. Homosexual behaviour can cause offence, polarise relationships, induce violence, and as a consequence morale and unit effectiveness can suffer.

Anyone who admits to, displays the orientation of, or indulges in homosexuality will be required to resign or be discharged.

Homosexual activity which is illegal under civil law or which has aggravated disciplinary features may also lead to prosecution.

(*The Discipline and Standards Paper*, MoD 1993; emphasis added).

With this brief paragraph the British Army *Discipline and Standards Paper* unambiguously classifies homosexual conduct as unacceptable. There is no further discussion of the subject, and no guidance or clarification is offered as to what constitutes evidence that an Army member '. . . displays the orientation of' homosexuality. Presumably it is assumed that all heterosexuals innately recognise homosexuals, even without sexual propositioning. The Military Police, who investigate accusations of homosexuality made against soldiers, do have a set of characteristic behaviour patterns against which they measure alleged gay personnel, since they must necessarily produce evidence which can withstand legal cross-examination. Nevertheless, given the extremely serious consequences of asserting a member of the armed forces to be homosexual, it is surprising that the *Discipline and Standards Paper* fails to warn about the need to beware of malice in responding to what are often anonymous claims.

The British armed forces were exempted from the 1967 Sexual Offences Act, which decriminalised certain forms of homosexual behaviour between consenting partners aged 21 or over. Potential recruits are encouraged to disclose their sexual orientation and warned that homosexual activity within the Services remains a dismissable offence.

Considerable publicity was given to the publication in August 1994 of Ministry of Defence data on the numbers of homosexuals dismissed from the British armed forces. From January 1990–May 1994, 260 personnel were discharged or administratively dismissed. The breakdown by Service and rank was:

	Royal Navy	Army	RAF
	2 Chaplains	4 Majors	1 Sqn Leader
	2 Lt Cmdrs	4 Captains	2 Flt Lieuts
	4 CPOs	1 Lieutenant	3 Fl. Offcrs
	3 POs	1 Warrant Offcr	4 Sergeants
	3 Ld. Ratings	3 Sergeants	16 Corporals
	35 Ratings	8 Corporals	26 Snr Aircrafts(wo)men
		17 L. Cpls	3 Leading Air(wo)men
		113 Privates	
TOTALS	49	151	55

The Ministry of Defence insisted on its continued legal entitlement to dismiss homosexual Servicemen and women, denied
that any policy changes were imminent and refuted sugges-
tions that it would be forced by the European Court to pay out
huge compensation claims for loss of employment. Whilst the
MoD acknowledged that British employment law provided protection for various groups of people – including the disabled
and pregnant women – it reaffirmed its view '. . . that it is not
illegal to a dismiss a gay person from the Services since the
European Directive on equal treatment contained an exemption for matters affecting national security.' (Ministry of
Defence spokesperson, *The Guardian*, 6 August 1994.)

Of the 64 dismissed from the Army between January
1993–May 1994, 33 were women, suggesting that lesbians continue to receive disproportionate investigative treatment, as
they constitute only 7% of Army strength. That women are
particularly subject to inquiry and at a greater risk of being
discharged is supported by American evidence that women are
2½ times more likely than men to be sacked from the Navy for
homosexuality (quoted in Enloe, *op. cit.*). Much expensive
Services police time is spent interviewing suspected lesbians in
order to encourage voluntary confessions, and seeking the identity of accomplices – fellow lesbians who can be 'outed' at the
same time for the price of one investigation. Elaine Chambers,
then a member of the WRAC, reported in the national press in
1994 how such cases were handled by the British Army police
team – the Special Investigation Branch – in 1988. Her Army
accommodation – she was a nurse – was rigorously examined
by the police. Personal possessions, such as diaries, letters,
photographs and videotapes, were systematically removed and
analysed for clues which would incriminate the owner as a les-
bian. Lengthy interrogations followed in which attention was
constantly focused by the SIB on acquaintances of Elaine's
who might also prove worthy of investigation.

Elaine Chambers was exonerated of the charge initially
brought against her – one of assaulting another woman – but
she was judged guilty of lesbianism and dismissed from the
Army, although there was never any suggestion that she was

professionally incompetent or failed to meet the terms of her nursing contract.

In November 1993 a Channel Four TV programme on the work of the RN police entitled 'Navy Blues' documented the determined pursuit of a sailor suspected of homosexuality. Anonymous allegations led to RN detectives interrogating a sonar operator about his sexual orientation. His denial of homosexuality was not accepted. As with the Chambers case, personal belongings were seized and examined. A list of what proved to be contact numbers for gay pubs was discovered amongst his possessions. Confronted with this evidence, the sailor confessed to homosexual inclinations, though strenuously denied ever importuning any naval personnel. This denial was accepted by the RN police and the disciplinary panel subsequently convened to consider the matter. The sailor was dismissed – made redundant at a time of high unemployment for demonstrating homosexual affiliations, even though there were no complaints from immediate colleagues and no suggestion of homosexual involvement with any colleagues in the Navy.

Arising from this particular case is an appeal to the European Court. Irrespective of the specific outcome, it is certain that British exclusionary policy will be subject to increasing challenge through international tribunals. European Union equal opportunities legislation has had costly consequences for the UK armed forces (see Chapter 5), especially since such legislation has been held to apply retrospectively to policies applied to pregnant members by the Services. Maintaining a policy of excluding homosexuals from the armed forces may prove similarly vulnerable to legal judgments, and equally expensive in terms of subsequent compensation for loss of career. The European Convention on Human Rights – which guarantees the right to privacy and to family life – is likely ultimately to constitute the basis of a successful challenge to current UK policy.

An immediate practical concern to taxpayers is the waste of resources that inevitably follows from a policy requiring all homosexuals to be dismissed from the Service. Combining both recruitment, basic and specialist training costs produces a substantial investment total. The amount varies considerably depending on the particular specialism pursued. A fast-jet pilot, for example, costs upwards of £5m spent before achieving professional competency. A sonar operator is less expensive, but the result of dismissing 260 British Service personnel as homosexual between 1990–94 must be an effective loss of at least £70m to the taxpayer.

In Britain the Ministry of Defence has shown no sign of wanting to amend its policy of rigorously excluding homosexuals from the armed forces.* Moreover, the Services' own internal police systems continue to spend time and resources pursuing and challenging suspected homosexuals, although if proven the outcome is now likely to be dismissal alone rather than a combination of criminal charges followed by dismissal. Nevertheless, loss of employment itself constitutes a major punishment, and there are indicators suggesting that the current hardline MoD policy may soon cease to be sustainable.

In June 1995 four ex-Service personnel (three men and one woman) succeeded in obtaining a judicial review by the High Court of their dismissal from military employment solely on the grounds of their confessed homosexuality. The applicants were seeking a ruling that the British legal system had authority to invoke European Union human rights legislation to supervene MoD policy. All four litigants had exemplary Service records, and there was no suggestion that their sexual orientation had interfered with or prejudiced their professional competence. Nor had there been any objections from colleagues as to their continued employment in the armed forces. What the applicants wanted was reinstatement in their jobs once the High Court had ruled that British policy in banning homosexuals *per se* from military employment was illegal in terms of the relevant European Union convention.

The Court's ruling was that it did have jurisdiction to consider the issue, but concluded that the MoD was acting lawfully in discharging personnel because of a homosexual orientation. The two judges agreed that this was essentially a matter for the

*This remains true despite the apparently concessionary establishment by the Ministry of Defence in the autumn of 1995 of an internal committee to review its exclusionary policy.

British Parliament to decide, that such an opportunity would arise during the five-yearly review of the Armed Forces Act in 1996, and that current MoD policy could only be overturned by the Court if it could be shown to be 'irrational'. One of the judges expressed considerable sympathy with the applicants, however, commenting: 'While The Ministry's arguments might seem unconvincing, they could not be dismissed as outrageously defying logic.' (Lord Justice Simon Brown). He concluded 'with hesitation and regret' that the armed forces did have the law on their side.

In light of the more relaxed attitude to the continued employment of homosexuals in the American forces, the tough exclusionary line currently pursued by the British MoD looks increasingly fragile. Moreover, there have been significant shifts in the policies of other armed forces on this issue which isolate the British position still further.

Of course, in the past the United Kingdom has been by no means unique in declaring homosexuality and membership of the armed forces to be incompatible. The most comprehensive study of military policies towards homosexuality was undertaken by Stanley Harris and reported in *The Journal of Homosexuality*, 1991. Harris surveyed military attachés in 110 non-communist embassies in Washington. Fifty-seven responded. Of these:

- 28 reported no policy on homosexual behaviour and armed forces membership;
- 21 reported policies excluding homosexuals; and
- 8 reported policies accepting homosexual and bisexual people

However, by 1994 many of these countries had changed their policies towards homosexuals serving in the armed forces. Australia, Belgium, Canada, France, Israel, the Netherlands, Spain and New Zealand no longer exclude or dismiss gays. Indeed, the Dutch have recently introduced an initiative under which homosexual men may discuss potential areas of concern with heterosexual colleagues with the intention of reducing homophobia and allaying anxieties about working with gay colleagues.

Moreover, the highly publicised manoeuvring over President Clinton's 1992 election campaign promise to lift the ban on homosexuals in the American armed forces has kept the issue in the public eye in America. Although removing the exclusion of gay personnel has proved difficult to achieve in the face of Service and Congressional opposition, significant changes have occurred. From February 1994 a 'don't ask, don't tell' policy was introduced which denied to the US Services the right to enquire into the sexual orientation of its members, though it still permitted the discharge of those who made their homosexuality known. The immediate consequence has been a dramatic fall in the numbers dismissed – only 279 between October 1993–August 1994, compared with an annual average of around 1,000 during the 1980–92 period. The right to dismiss remains subject to perennial challenge in the American courts – so far unsuccessfully – but the constitutional legitimacy of the new policy has also been questioned. Only a decision by the US Supreme Court seems capable of resolving the issues. The United Kingdom appears to be increasingly isolated in its adamant refusal to amend its exclusion and dismissal policies.

Most research into the practical outcomes of seeking to exclude homosexuals from the military has been conducted in the United States. One study by Joseph Harry published in *The Journal of Homosexuality*, 1984, suggested that such policies failed completely. In 'Homosexual Men and Women Who Served Their Country', Harry compared the percentage of homosexuals who had served in the armed forces with a matched heterosexual sample. Interview data on 1,456 recruits from 1969–70 showed that homosexual and heterosexual men were equally likely to have served, and that lesbians were more likely to have been members of the Services than their civilian counterparts. One explanation for this offered by Harry is that at the time of enlistment, recruits may be unaware of their homosexuality. Such a view is entirely consistent with examinations of the development of sexuality amongst adolescents within Western cultures. That youthful recruits may be uncertain as to their sexual preferences, and willing to experiment, should not therefore come as much of a surprise. It does, however, explain how recruits can honestly deny anything other than heterosexual interests when challenged by recruiters.

A more recent study by Judith Stiehm in *The University of Miami Law Review*, 1992, traces the evolution of US exclusionary policy towards homosexuals, focusing particularly on the way policy has been modified in the light of recent political and legal developments. Like Harry, Stiehm concludes that in practice attempts to ban homosexuals do not work, and that such a policy may possibly be counterproductive in military terms in that it restricts the deployability of suspect individuals.

Major cultural changes in attitudes towards homosexuality have occurred within Britain since 1967, and the reluctance of the armed forces to make any concessions is increasingly idiosyncratic. Other social institutions which also involve working in close physical proximity and an operational imperative of effective teamwork – such as the police and fire services – do not exclude homosexuals from their ranks. Indeed, gay policemen can share their police houses with homosexual partners. Although there remains a substantial and hostile undertow of prejudice to homosexuals within such macho organisations, both the police and fire services have come to terms with the legal impossibility of pursuing a policy of exclusion, and found that their services have neither collapsed nor been seriously eroded in terms of public confidence.

The argument advanced by the MoD – that the unique working circumstances of British armed forces members must necessarily exclude homosexuals – looks progressively suspect. Not only will they in all probability eventually fall at a legal hurdle – in Europe if not in Britain, and with subsequent costly compensation claims for wrongful dismissal confronting the MoD – but the experience of the emergency services such as ambulance, fire and police agencies suggests that the operational capabilities of the Services would not be threatened if the current policy of excluding homosexuals was abandoned. The argument that licensing homosexuality is a charter for bullies – a common defence for present British policy – does not stand close examination. Gay men or women might use superior rank to force junior personnel into unwanted sexual associations, but the same is equally true of heterosexuals, and such conduct, regardless of sexual orientation, is already clearly forbidden by Service disciplinary codes. Transgressors are vulnerable not only to discovery and punishment by the chain of command, but also to being denounced by victims increasingly aware that sexual harassment is no longer officially sanctioned.

In any case, importuning remains a sexual offence in the UK, and Services personnel thus already have a defence against unwanted sexual advances from colleagues (whether heterosexual or homosexual). Removing the ban on homosexuals within the military would:

- recognise that this policy is in any case ineffective;
- permit gay individuals to engage in homosexual activity outside (or by mutual consent with a partner within) the military community;
- remove the threat of blackmail which is a real possibility in the current situation; and
- openly acknowledge that sexual orientation has no bearing on professional military competence.

If such a change was considered too revolutionary, a policy modification which permitted homosexuals to continue serving providing they confined their sexual activities to locations outside their military environment would at least have the advantage of reducing the losses incurred in expensive training and might constitute a sufficient *modus vivendi* to eliminate the threat of substantial compensation payments as the result of European social policy.

HOMOPHOBIA

However, underlying policies excluding homosexuals from the UK armed forces are important psychological constructs which, consciously or otherwise, affect the attitudes of policy-makers within defence Ministries. The depth of hostility to accepting homosexuals within the military – not only at the policy production level but amongst the rank and file as well – indicates clearly just how powerful are the psychological influences involved. Anti-gay jokes and a rejection of anything other than an overt heterosexuality constitute the daily cultural normality for Services members. There is no evidence of any encouragement for Servicemen to engage in 'queer bashing' – assaults on known or suspected homosexuals – but the prevailing sentiment towards gays remains dismissive and condemnatory.

Yet the history of world warfare contains many accounts of homosexual warriors. Alexander the Great, Julius Caesar, Richard the Lionheart – a notorious paederast – and Frederick the Great do not appear to have suffered military disadvantage or disloyalty from their followers because they were not heterosexual. Warlike Sparta operated on the principle that soldiers were less likely to flee the battlefield if their (male) lovers were beside them – indeed, sometimes such pairs were chained together to discourage any unauthorised retreat.

However, the fact that homosexuality is perceived in such a bellicose way in military communities suggests it also represents a threat to those rejecting it. Freud observed that it was an anatomical fact that in all males and females there are traces of the apparatus of the other sex. Anatomically there may have been an original predisposition to bisexuality, which in the course of the development of the human species has largely been altered to monosexuality (Sigmund Freud, *Three Contributions to the Theory of Sex*, 1962). Although collected a long time ago, the data in the Kinsey Reports (A C Kinsey *et al.*, *Sexual Behaviour in the Human Male*, 1948, and *Sexual Behaviour in the Human Female*, 1953) suggests that sexual attraction to same-sex adults is relatively common. Kinsey concluded that the world is not divided into exclusive heterosexual and homosexual communities. Instead, people can be placed on a continuum according to their sexual preferences and behaviour. According to his study, 28% of adult women and 50% of adult males acknowledged at least one occasion on which they had been aroused homosexually, although the great majority considered themselves to be – and behaved as – heterosexuals. Only about 2% of females and 4% of males defined themselves as exclusively homosexual both in preference and sexual activity. Experiencing some degree of physical attraction from somebody of the same sex is thus not particularly unusual in adult life.

During childhood and adolescence it is widely accepted that emotional interests are predominantly directed towards members of the same sex. Anthony Storr comments:

> . . . in many instances, this homosexual interest may persist until early adult life without there being anything abnormal or unusual about it. Homosexuality in the sense of a fixed adult pattern of behaviour cannot be said to exist until the middle twenties; for often the pattern spontaneously alters and the person becomes heterosexual long after the legal age of maturity has been attained.
> (Anthony Storr, *The Integrity of the Personality*, 1960)

Given the high proportion of the armed forces who fall within the age structure referred to by Storr, it would not be surprising to find a substantial proportion undecided as to their eventual sexual orientation. Yet they live in a society in which official abhorrence and rejection of homosexuality is endorsed and from which they will be expelled, losing their careers, should they themselves discover that they are gay. Homosexuality thus becomes something to fear: an insidious threat to be dispelled by very public denials, mockery and disdain and overt demonstrations of heterosexuality whenever possible.

Historically the armed forces have offered the most undiluted image of masculinity and machismo. Serving in the armed forces has therefore been particularly attractive *and reinforcing* to men wishing to demonstrate their undeniable maleness. The introduction of Servicewomen – particularly into operational and command roles – has, of course, already menaced the stability of this desired world-view, but acknowledging the legitimacy of homosexuality is even more challenging, since it requires the recognition that even the toughest action-man has female components within his personality.

All human beings comprise a mixture of male and female elements whatever our gender. Whether it is the male or female components which dominate our personalities is determined largely by cultural factors such as our families of origin and our exposure to socially approved gender roles, which we are encouraged to emulate. Because homosexuality is identified by many heterosexual males as effeminate – and therefore 'weak' – tolerating it is especially difficult for those individuals who wish to deny the feminine side of their personality and to emphasise only their rampant masculinity. It may be that such obsessively machismo-minded people are attracted to employment within the armed forces precisely because it offers support for their denial of any internal femininity. Accepting homosexuality means coming to terms with the female side of male nature and attacks the comforting belief that true men are men, women are completely different and that the only proper meeting point is in heterosexuality.

Nearly 50 years ago the sociologist Theo Adorno and his colleagues put forward a theory of the *authoritarian personality*. Such a person exhibited prejudice because of certain personality traits towards minority groups – ethnic, racial or other 'out' groups (T W Adorno *et al.*, *The Authoritarian Personality*, New York, 1950). Adorno's major concern was with understanding the development of anti-semitism. His research on white, middle-class Americans introduced measures designed to evaluate this, as well as 'ethno-centrism' (the belief that one's own ethnic or membership group is superior to others). Out of this emerged Adorno's 'F' scale – F for Fascism – which sought to measure anti-democratic tendencies. Anti-semitism was found to be part of a general constellation of attitudes rather than a single prejudice, so that the authoritarian personality was seen to be prejudiced in a generalised way: 'Typically, the authoritarian personality is hostile to people of inferior status, servile to those of higher status, contemptuous of weakness, rigid and inflexible, intolerant of ambiguity and uncertainty, unwilling to introspect feelings and an upholder of conventional values and ways of life.' (In *Psychology: the Science of Mind and Behaviour*, by Richard Gross; London: Hodder & Stoughton, 1987.)

Critics of the authoritarian personality theory challenged Adorno on the grounds that his work was simply a disguised attack on people holding right-wing political views, and that there could be equivalent authoritarianism on the left. More generally, H Brown in *People Groups and Society*, (Milton Keynes: Open University Press, 1985) argued that: '. . . cultural or societal norms may be much more important than personality in accounting for ethno-centrism, out-group rejection, prejudice and discrimination.' Contrary to what the theory of the authoritarian personality would predict, anti-black attitudes in the southern USA have not been combined with anti-semitism or prejudice against other minority groups. The localised nature of hostility towards particular groups can instead be explained better in terms of social conformity. The need to conform and not to be seen as different will cause active discrimination against minorities which are perceived as deviant.

Branding members of the armed forces in a generalised way as 'authoritarian personalities' is simplistic nonsense. No doubt some Service personnel would score quite highly on Adorno's F scale – but so too would some politicians, journalists, teachers, doctors and business leaders. Attitudes associated with inflexible political and social views are not unique to the military. A more credible explanation for homophobia within the armed forces is the emphasis on social conformity – which requires such a response – together with the very real threat of career damage if any other attitude is expressed.

Summary

Military authorities in Britain and the USA have attempted to control patterns of sexual behaviour and direct sexual energies into approved channels. The continuation of such policies seems increasingly improbable since they fail to recognise fundamental changes in matters of human sexuality and operate in ways which discriminate against a group – homosexuals – whose conduct has become increasingly decriminalised and more widely accepted in both societies. Intervention in choice of marital partner and efforts to outlaw certain types of consensual liaison also run counter to contemporary expectations of personal choice. Military communities cannot pretend to be immune to the consequences of sexual revolutions.

CHAPTER 8

The Metamorphosis of Military Communities: The World of Work

The end of the Cold War, developments in weapons technology and the extended range of operational roles now performed by women within the military have brought about unprecedented change for the armed forces. At the same time, many of the traditional social structures which have been employed by military institutions both to support and control their members have become obsolete and unacceptable. How must military organisations evolve in order to adapt themselves successfully in such mercurial times?

This chapter discusses:

- probable changes in location and housing for armed forces members arising from the repatriation of American and British Service personnel to their home countries;
- predicted patterns of unaccompanied Service (and therefore marital separation);
- the consequences on military appointments of a more vigorous application of equal opportunities principles;
- the imminent requirement to provide within all armed forces post-trauma support and stress counselling; and
- matters affecting the morale and motivation of military employees where the undeniable risks of this particular form of

employment are no longer compensated for through job security.

It is obvious that the wide range of simultaneous changes which our armed forces are undergoing at present implies the emergence of very different organisations in the near future. By the year 2000, military bodies will bear little relation in terms of size, geographical disposition and gender balance to their forerunners of even 25 years ago.

However, it is not only in the deployment of professional skills that military communities will rapidly bear little resemblance to their predecessors. Metamorphosis will occur across all dimensions of military societies. Fundamental adaptations to social and community structures will have to occur in recognition of contemporary family dynamics and the support systems required by staff combining a military career with marital and parental ambitions. These issues will be the focus of the next Chapter.

THE BOYS (AND GIRLS) ARE COMING HOME . . .

Until 1990, approximately one-third of the British armed forces were located outside the UK. Similarly, a comparable proportion of US forces were also permanently deployed outside the continental United States. For the foreseeable future, the end of the Cold War is bringing this distribution of military personnel to an end too. Global politico-military strategies no longer dictate the permanent stationing of substantial numbers of troops at key points where ideologies collide. Instead, for the armed forces, the enemy has shifted and threats now appear from different directions: Treasury pressures to reduce costs and declare peace dividends. Overseas bases, with their concomitant medical, educational, housing and other services, are natural targets for cost-cutting.

The budgetary economies gained from shutting overseas bases are not themselves obtained without cost. Returning personnel to America or Britain has involved redundancies – for which some financial compensation is unavoidable – and also raises issues about housing families. The British Army, for example, avoided the housing consequences of the substantial increase in the proportion of soldiers who married by locating large numbers of them outside the UK at any one time. Their housing requirements were, in effect, exported, so reducing the numbers of military houses which had to be provided at home. Returning British families, particularly from Germany, has produced difficulties for Army housing authorities. Stock, sometimes regardless of refurbishment need, has been necessarily pressed into use to cope with the exodus. In addition, because of the unavailability of appropriate housing in specific locations, returning Army families have been obliged to rent housing from civilian landlords, with Army funds supplementing the difference between married quarter charges and open market rentals in the form of Excess Rent Allowances.

These are, of course, short-term costs arising from relocation decisions. Viewed over a longer time-frame, some savings will accrue as the armed forces are reduced in size. However, there will not necessarily be any economies in the provision of accommodation. Although the British Army, for example, by 1999 will be 25–30% smaller than its 1989 establishment, a larger proportion – and a greater absolute number – of military families will be located in Britain. If the Army were to continue a policy of offering subsidised rented housing to all married personnel, its accommodation bill would rise substantially.

In fact, the creation of the tri-Service Defence Housing Executive in 1994 marked a significant portent. Although in the immediate future, the provision of married quarters remains the approved course, in the longer term it is clear that major changes in military housing are under way. Although initial attempts to privatise the entire portfolio of military housing – some 70,000 houses and flats – failed, there is little doubt that this represents the Treasury's preferred option. Transferring housing management either to housing associations or commercial landlords will have serious implications for rent subsidies. Historically, married quarter charges have been set so that the average rent paid equalled 70% of the average rent levels of local authority social housing. But local authorities have become less important as providers within the housing market since this rent relationship was established. Moreover, the practice of providing subsidy for all local authority tenants has long since disappeared. The Defence Housing Executive is unlikely to continue indiscriminate subsidisation to *all* military families, irrespective of rank or household income, simply because they live in married quarters. The justification for such subsidies – that they reflected the turbulent and uncertain nature of military life – should arguably be more properly reflected in salaries and conditions of service. Certainly, future managers of military housing, whether as agents of or successors to the Defence Housing Executive, will pursue rent-charging practices more in line with those followed by housing associations. The net effect will be that rent levels will rise. The extra cost could, of course, be borne by the Ministry of Defence rather than passed on to the occupants of military accommodation. However, it is more probable that higher rents will eventually impact directly on the families themselves.

Rising rent charges for married quarters will act as additional encouragement to Service families to choose their own accommodation. Predominantly this will be through house purchase. Despite the collapse of the housing market since 1990, the attractions of property ownership are deeply embedded in the British psyche and there are severe limitations on the availability of satisfactory rented alternatives. The permanent relocation in the UK of the greater part of the Army and Royal Air Force in any case produces a strong incentive for increasing the rates of house ownership within those organisations. Although turbulence within the home country will still be a feature of British military life, it does not constitute such a barrier to house purchase as overseas deployment. For the United States, however, there are substantive differences. The very size of America means that national postings may still be thousands of miles away from kin or home territory. House purchase decisions may well therefore be deferred until the end of military employment.

Increased rates of home ownership amongst serving military families will come about, therefore, partly because a window of opportunity to adopt the prevailing patterns of house tenure in Britain has suddenly opened, but also because actual or anticipated rent rises act as an incentive to leave military housing. The potential disengagement of older, more mature families from married quarters has important social implications for the nature of military communities which are discussed later.

MARITAL SEPARATION RATES

Professional armed forces of necessity are committed to life-long learning: they represent *par excellence* a process of continuing education. This process begins with basic induction training and persists to the end of a military career. It involves both theoretical learning and its practical application, often in the form of training exercises. Whatever the format, the training process has hitherto normally involved marital separation, and only for very lengthy courses is accommodation for spouses provided. Thus, the permanent education requirements compelled by unremitting technological change have inevitably added to the amount of separation experienced by married couples in the armed forces. Indeed, at certain ages, training constitutes the principal cause of separation.

Size reductions in British and American Services will not reduce the drive to update skills and knowledge. Whilst some predictions about armed forces of the future are more speculative, the requirement that the highest levels of technical proficiency be sustained is a matter of certainty, not fanciful prophecy. Continuous training will remain a prominent feature of military life. It will also remain a major cause of marital separation, albeit often of a short-term nature. Nevertheless, interruptions to conjoint relationships – whatever their length – interfere with preferred marriage patterns, as Chapter 1 illustrated. Providing, or paying for, accommodation for spouses during training courses is an option military institutions may consider, but it is unlikely that this approach will command widespread favour. In any case, the dispersal of armed forces families into house ownership within civilian communities will limit the number of spouses who would be available to accompany partners undergoing training. To achieve optimum human resource management, a more effective approach would be to ensure that techniques for coping with separation permeate throughout Service communities – and that training and exercises as well as unaccompanied deployments are *all* recognised as constituting forms of separation.

Separation itself must become a process for which individuals receive training. Of course, the panoply of Family Centers, Welfare Advice and other support services functioning within British and American military institutions offers valuable help to couples, but it is primarily *reactive*, responding to difficulties and miseries which have already materialised. Educating families about successful separation management is a *pro-active* policy which seeks to avoid problems arising. Such an educational initiative started in the British Army in 1994 with the distribution of a short but user-friendly and invitingly produced booklet on *Homecoming*. This focuses specifically on the reintegration into the family of the absentee, acknowledging that after even short separations homecoming needs to be planned. Readers are encouraged to reflect on:

How to Prepare for a Happy Homecoming

Talking about your feelings is an important part of preparing for a happy homecoming.

Wives/partners	Service members	Children
may be thinking:	*may wonder:*	*wonder:*
How much has he changed?	Will my family still need me?	How long will Dad stay?
Have I made the right decisions while he was away?	Will the children recognise me?	Will the rules change at home?
Will I see less of my friends now?	Will the family be happy to see me again?	Will I get punished because I was naughty sometimes?

Realism is encouraged. Readers are invited to recognise that:

Everyone Changes. It's only natural that children, wives, partners, husbands, family and friends change with time. They won't be exactly as you remembered them.

Communication May Be Difficult at First. As everyone has changed, it will take a little while for people to get to know each other again.

Roles Have Changed. A wife may have learned a lot about managing a home. A husband may have new job-skills and added responsibilities. (British Army 1994: authorship unknown)

Improving the ability of families to manage separation should be identified as a key task, for separation is likely to increase rather than diminish. In addition to a demanding training schedule which interrupts family togetherness, no substantial reduction in unaccompanied postings can be anticipated with certainty in the immediate future. The political developments in Ireland in the mid-1990s may reduce the demand for British forces to serve in the North, but commitments to the United Nations, NATO and the Allied Rapid Reaction Corps could easily outweigh this. For both Britain and America, support for the UN and membership of various politico-military alliances presage unpredictable consequences in terms of armed forces deployment. It is abundantly clear, however, that military engagements of this nature will mean separation from spouses and families.

In May 1995, the British Secretary of State for Defence announced the formation of a permanent joint headquarters to take control of all peacekeeping and humanitarian operations. Also promised were new air-portable vehicles and satellite communications enabling a rapid reaction force – built around airborne and commando units – to complement NATO's multinational reaction forces. Such developments were clearly based on the premise that Britain's armed forces could anticipate a turbulent future in which they would be almost continuously engaged in peacekeeping operations to some degree.

Moreover, if British participation in forces stationed in mainland Europe was also to become unaccompanied, the incidence of marital separation would rise dramatically. The pressure to convert overseas service on the European continent to unaccompanied status is entirely economic. Without families present, there would be no need for military authorities to provide education, health, social work and retail support services. Similar calculations apply to the United States in many of the overseas locations where personnel will continue to be stationed. Any economies which can be achieved in this way will, of course, be largely at the expense of family and marital stability. This may well be judged by the chain of command too serious a threat to operational efficiency, and therefore too high a price to pay, to warrant the savings which might be forthcoming from ending accompanied overseas tours. However, the decisions are likely to be made by politicians rather than generals, and the deciding factor may well be cost rather than armed forces morale and retention rates.

On balance, it seems probable that marital separation will increase rather than fall in the near future. To avoid such a development damaging motivation and operational readiness, suitable support systems for partners and families must form a prominent part of the Services' own employee care and welfare agencies.

THE IRRESISTIBLE RISE OF EQUAL OPPORTUNITIES

In February 1994, the United States Air Force issued the following memorandum:

Command Responsibility for Equal Opportunity
ACTION MEMORANDUM

In today's quality Air Force, the contributions of each member become increasingly important. Accordingly, we must ensure that all our people are given the opportunity to reach their full potential. Air Force policy on equal opportunity is straightforward: military members and civilian employees will be provided equal opportunity and treatment regardless of age, color, national origin, race, religion, sex, or, in the case of civilian employees, disabling conditions.

As we continue to downsize and reorganize the force, we must value and protect our most important resource – people. People must be treated fairly, with dignity and respect, and be measured by their performance. Our commitment to equal opportunity is an integral part of leadership and a responsibility shared by all Air Force leaders. It is essential to readiness and the right thing to do.

The document was signed by the USAF Chief of Staff and the Secretary of the Air Force. It was thus a reiteration at the highest command level of policy and intent. In Britain, all the armed forces proclaim adherence to a policy of equal opportunity. As mentioned earlier (Chap 5), in October 1994 the British Ministry of Defence announced the creation of a new Directorate for Equal Opportunities, located within the Army Manning Branch and headed by a full Colonel. The first holder of this post was in fact female. Its remit is to monitor: 'racial, religious and female issues' (*Soldier*, October 1994).

The establishment of such a unit is of more than symbolic importance. It represents an awareness that equal opportunity issues do not by-pass military institutions but must be seriously addressed. It will also act as an advisory agency for the Army, enabling it to avoid illegal employment practices – such as the discharge of pregnant Servicewomen – which have had expensive repercussions. Details of progress achieved in equal opportunities by gender have been reviewed earlier (in Chapter 5). Even those barriers which still remain – such as the exclusion of women from infantry or tank roles, and from direct ground combat in the USA – look vulnerable. Divergent NATO practices mean that within the alliance the range of activities considered operationally feasible for women vary considerably. Norway, for example, does not exclude women from any military role, and in Denmark women entered what were previously male-only combat roles in 1988. The Committee on Women in NATO Forces (a cross-national association of senior Servicewomen) has adopted the stance that whilst women may *choose* not to seek incorporation in combat roles, the choice should be theirs and not determined by discriminatory exclusions or taboos. It seems therefore unlikely that the floodgates of combat-hardened female veterans are about to open. But the proportion of Servicewomen who do emerge as combat-trained and experienced must reflect their own decisions and professional competences, not customs and conventions grounded on chauvinism and bigotry rather than merit.

The commitment to promote equal opportunities for all racial groups may involve the new Army Directorate in very controversial findings. Ethnic monitoring is still relatively recent in the British Services. The results for the British Army showed that in 1992/3 only 1.3% of applicants and 0.8% of recruits were classified as non-white. Reflecting on this *Soldier* magazine commented:

> Racism is not a major problem in the British Army. It is a serious issue, however, and one which the Army is tackling positively. It is widely felt that the Armed Forces should reflect the ethnic composition of the society they serve. While they are unlikely ever to mirror the precise ethnic mix, they should at least aim to be highly representative of the nation.
>
> (*Soldier*, October 1994)

To encourage applications from ethnic minorities, Army recruiters are receiving ethnic sensitivity training under a team headed by a former USAF officer, and the Ministry of Defence published *Race Relations: A Code of Practice* in December 1993 which spelled out: 'action to be taken against personnel found guilty of racial discrimination, abuse or other ill-treatment.' Nevertheless, with ethnic minority groups constituting around 5% of the UK population, they remain significantly under-represented in the armed forces at present. Although no evidence of systematic discrimination on racial grounds exists, anecdotal accounts of prejudice and discrimination affecting promotion or entry into élite units abound. Even members of the British Royal Family have decided it necessary to comment publicly on the absence of ethnic minorities within certain British Army regiments, and Prince Charles has been personally involved in at least one case which led to compensation being paid where an Army Board of Enquiry accepted that racial discrimination had occurred.

In June 1995 the British Commission on Racial Equality revealed that premier regiments of the British Army – the

Household Cavalry, which comprises some of the oldest and most prestigious units – excluded applicants from ethnic minorities seeking to transfer in from other regiments. Effectively black soldiers were screened out from joining, whatever their proven military competence. In practice, a very small number of black recruits have succeeded in joining the Household Cavalry – six were known to be so engaged at mid-1995 – but the experience of the first black Grenadier Guardsman suggests the process is extremely difficult, as he resigned after three years of what he described as 'racial taunts'. The consultants hired by the Ministry of Defence to raise ethnic awareness sensitivity have themselves commented: 'The Army is trying hard, but what it fails to understand is why anyone should want to join an organization where they are going to get called a nig-nog.' (Jerome Mack of *Equality Associates* quoted in *The Independent*, 18 June 1995).

There appear to be considerable cultural differences both within and between each of the British Services as to the social acceptance and professional integration – as measured by promotion – of non-white personnel. The RAF appears to be the most open Service, accepting and using relevant skills and talents whatever the owner's skin colour, and the highest level of rank seniority achieved by ethnic minority members has been in the RAF. In contrast, selection into certain units within the Army appears almost impossible for non-white applicants.

The application of equal opportunities policies to ethnic minorities is still at a preliminary stage within the British armed forces. This contrasts markedly with the American position. Since President Truman issued an executive order in 1948 establishing equal opportunities within the US military, race relations have been widely perceived as superior inside the Services to those of civilian society. US research findings suggest that the military is viewed as a favourable, or at least neutral, work environment by most blacks; that ethnic minority males who are veterans gain economic advantages over non-veterans; and that disadvantaged black high school youth recognise the military as a channel of social mobility. However, ethnic origin is still seen in some research as accounting for a proportionate under-representation of blacks at certain promotion levels. (For a review of ethnic equal opportunities progress within the American Army, see 'Racial Inequality in Army Promotions' by David R. Segal *et al.*, in *The Journal of Political and Military Sociology*, Spring 1979.)

In Britain, less unequivocal progress can be demonstrated for ethnic groups in the Services. Although the establishment of an equal opportunities unit in the Army was widely perceived as a belated but appropriate response to the need to attend to issues of *gender* inequality, in practice the matter of racial discrimination may prove to be the area in which the Directorate identifies recruitment and promotion practices which must change to ensure that the armed forces remain within the law.

It is a safe prediction that by the year 2000, equal opportunity policies will have brought about a multitude of changes in the gender and racial composition of the UK armed forces at all levels, transformations which some of its present members will find both startling and unwelcome.

STRESS: EMPLOYMENT IMPLICATIONS FOR
THE ARMED FORCES

Britain and America have both become increasingly litigious societies. Citizens who have suffered damage to their health or impairment of function are encouraged to pursue financial compensation claims. In the USA, the existence of lawyers willing to work on a 'no win, no fee' basis has escalated personal injury claims and raised enormously the premiums demanded of doctors by insurance companies to protect them against allegations of negligence. So far in Britain, 'no win, no fee' legal practice is relatively uncommon. Moreover, the government itself effectively reduces the value of any compensation settlement by deducting from it social security benefit paid from the date a compensation action is initiated. As it may take anything up to two years for a Court to arrive at a decision, substantial benefit receipts can build up and significantly erode the value of any compensation actually received. Nevertheless, experiments with lawyers charging clients no fees unless compensation is achieved have begun in Britain, and claims from people alleging damaged health and capacities are unlikely to fall.

In 1994 an English social worker successfully sued his former employer on the grounds that the stress induced by the employer's working practices had damaged his health (Walker v. Northumberland County Council). Unlike the long-standing Industrial Injuries scheme – which compensates individuals for personal injuries or accidents arising out of employment – this case was significant for a number of reasons. First, it did not arise in employment circumstances recognised as potentially threatening to health, such as work in mining, building or farming, for example. Secondly, what was judged to have brought about ill-health were the demands of an employer seeking to achieve pay-roll economies by reducing personnel and in consequence imposing intolerable pressure on staff remaining. This is an outcome which is widely acknowledged and recognised within the armed forces where it is frequently termed *overstretch*. Even before the post-Cold War redundancy programme began to have much impact, concern about overstretch was easy to discover within the Services. It was claimed that sustaining operational readiness and professional competence at the highest possible levels was incompatible with the number and variety of deployment obligations to which military institutions were committed by political decision. Certainly in the 1980s – when alternative employment opportunities were greater – there was some evidence that skilled personnel voluntarily departed from the Services and rejoined civilian life because work pressures had become intolerable. One result of this, of course, was that work burdens on those remaining became even harder. These processes were exacerbated by redundancy programmes in the 1990s which did not reduce operational obligations at the same rate and extent. Consequently, the incidence of overstretch allegedly increased, although now widespread economic recession severely limited alternative employment options, at least for British Service personnel. As a result, whilst *battlefield* or *post-trauma* stress has been gradually accepted as an area where military institutions must offer employee care programmes, non-trauma induced stress is just as likely to occur within 'downsized' armed forces as in the civilian world.

The commemorations in 1995 which marked the fiftieth

anniversaries of the end of the Second World War in Europe and in the Pacific highlighted the long-term consequences of battlefield exposure. Veterans of that conflict certainly suffered from the psychological repercussions of such experiences, but *Post-trauma Stress* was not a descriptive term recognised as applying to them until relatively recently. Instead, it was initially used only in relation to survivors from Vietnam, the Falklands War and the Gulf War: a late twentieth-century risk to which members of the armed forces were uniquely exposed.

Subsequently, post-trauma stress has come to be understood as a widespread condition, potentially afflicting any human beings irrespective of employment or historical context. It is hardly a new phenomenon; in the twentieth century there are many descriptions of what is now classified as post-trauma stress, particularly in the literature of the First World War. Nowhere is this concept more powerfully revealed than in the poetry of Wilfred Owen:

These are men whose minds the Dead have ravished.
Memory fingers in their hair of murders,
Multitudinous murders they once witnessed.
Wading sloughs of flesh these helpless wander,
Treading blood from lungs that had loved laughter.
Always they must see these things and hear them,
Batter of guns and shatter of flying muscles,
Carnage incomparable, and human squander
Rucked too thick for these men's extrication.

('Mental Cases' from *The Poems of Wilfred Owen*;
London: Chatto & Windus, 1990)

Post-traumatic Stress Disorder has been defined by the American Psychiatric Association as: 'The development of certain characteristic symptoms following a psychologically distressing event which is outside the range of normal human experience' (APA, *Diagnostic and Statistical Manual of Mental Disorders*, 1987). This begs the important question of what is 'normal', of course. In addition, human reactions to events which are unexpected, unwanted or shocking vary enormously so that it cannot be assumed that post-trauma stress inevitably follows exposure to a disturbing event. The episode which triggers responses labelled *disorder* may be objectively viewed as a slight accident or a major disaster. Whatever the initiating event, what matters to the survivor is that their coping abilities and normal life capacities subsequently become seriously disrupted; the trauma has led to a dysfunctional behaviour pattern which may be relatively mild or totally disabling.

The risks arising from exposure to trauma have been acknowledged throughout police, fire and ambulance services, as well as within the armed forces. Although for the latter, trauma is popularly identified with battlefield conflict, for many Service personnel harrowing incidents are more likely to arise from car accidents, training exercises and assistance to civil authorities during natural disasters. Some institutional resistance to the provision of post-trauma counselling within the British Services has been identified by Parkinson.

> The organization of the armed services provides an excellent basis on which to build a counselling and debriefing system, for extensive welfare support already exists. However, because of the macho image that is common, it is easy to believe that psychological debriefing is not necessary. This image is very strong, not only at the bottom, but throughout the services, where it can produce the response that only 'wets' and 'wimps' need help.
>
> (Frank Parkinson, *Post Trauma-Stress*;
> London: Sheldon Press, 1993)

However, hostility to the concept of post-trauma stress in the armed forces has diminished in Britain as a result of the 1982 Falklands War. Service psychiatrists have diagnosed and treated post-trauma stress generated by horrific experiences in that conflict, although not necessarily anticipating total cure. Surgeon Commander Morgan O'Connell of the British Royal Navy, one of the best known specialists in this field, has said:

> I tell every patient I see that there is no compensation for what they have been through. Damages for pain and loss, perhaps, but not

compensation. If people seek legal redress, that isn't going to cure them. For most there is no cure, all we can do is to help them live more comfortably with their scars.

(The Guardian, 8 February 1995)

The difficulties of obtaining effective medical intervention for post-trauma stress were lamented by Shakespeare in *Macbeth,* who is seeking a medical opinion about his wife's mental state:

Macbeth	How does your patient, doctor?

Doctor   Not so sick my lord,
As she is troubled with thick-coming fancies,
That keep her from her rest.

Macbeth   Cure her of that.
Canst thou not minister to a mind diseased,
Pluck from the memory a rooted sorrow,
Raze out the written troubles of the brain,
And with some sweet oblivious antidote
Cleansed the stuff'd bosom of that perilous stuff
Which weighs up on the heart?

Doctor   Therein the patient
Must minister to himself.

(Macbeth, Act V, Scene III)

In 1994 a British Army Sergeant successfully sued the Ministry of Defence for damage produced by undiagnosed and therefore untreated post-trauma stress caused by his involvement in the battle for Mount Tumbledown. Numerous similar cases are wending their way through the British Courts. A substantial bill may eventually confront the Defence Ministry. The MoD takes the problem seriously, and provides counselling and psychiatric support for Service personnel who are identified as suffering from post-trauma stress *whilst they are still serving.* But the condition does not necessarily manifest itself immediately, and disturbing flashbacks or other symptoms of maladaptive behaviour may not in any case be recognised as the aftermath of trauma until long after the sufferer has been discharged.

Some would argue, of course, that armed forces members must expect to face death, mutilation and destruction, that these are virtually features of their job specifications and that, as a result, there can be no justification for later complaint. Obviously employment within the Services does imply exposure to potentially distressing circumstances, and it would be blatantly unreasonable to sue for damages on this score alone, providing, of course, membership of the Services had been freely chosen. But plainly it can be contested that military employers, conscious of the effects which traumatic exposure may induce, have two clear duties:

- to warn employees as to the existence, symptoms and outcomes of post-trauma stress; and
- to provide a diagnostic and treatment service which actively searches for post-trauma victims rather than waits for self-referral.

In practice, what this amounts to is the kind of defensive management practice which civilian employers are obliged to undertake to ward off accusations of inadequate employee care: care which any reasonable employer could legitimately be expected to provide. The armed forces already offer an array of social welfare and psychiatric services which could be expected to spearhead post-trauma stress counselling. Where such support was not available from within, the Services would have to purchase suitable external expertise. Either method of managing post-trauma stress incurs costs, but failure to supply a pro-active approach will bring with it the risk of higher long-term financial settlements. Perhaps the key task is to educate staff throughout the chain of command about post-trauma stress so that awareness as to those situations in which it is the likely outcome can be heightened. The Ministry of Defence acknowledges the seriousness of post-trauma stress, and has publicly asserted that the matter is treated very seriously; and that when detected, the armed forces are well equipped to deal with it. However, a number of sufferers – primarily from the

The World of Work

Falklands and Gulf Wars – are seeking compensation for their condition, and their allegations consistently include the alleged failure on the part of the MoD to warn them of the possible danger and consequences of post-trauma stress.

WORK MOTIVATION AND THE ARMED FORCES:
ARE YOU WILLING TO DIE FOR THE UN?

Motives for joining – and staying in – military employment have always been mixed. Patriotism, variety of work, excellent training facilities, strong family links with the forces and travel opportunities have often been explanations proffered by recruits. The lack of alternative civilian employment has also been cited at times – though not by would-be recruits themselves – as an impelling factor. The sophisticated technology of contemporary warfare, however, means that military employers have insisted on higher educational standards, and the conventional assumption that if all other work avenues fail, the Services can be relied on to provide employment is no longer true. The armed forces of necessity have become highly selective in their recruitment and, as with other employers, candidates unable to demonstrate standard educational attainments or previous relevant job skills will experience great difficulty in being chosen.

Although recruits frequently complain about the discrepancy between the thrilling picture of Service life painted by the recruiting agents and the daily, less exotic, reality, there has until recently been an underlying expectation about military employment which had remained unchallenged. This was that working in the Services guaranteed job security – not, of course, for life, but at least for that period of years for which a contract of military employment was normal. In practice, the length of a typical career in the armed forces has varied quite considerably between the different Services. Nevertheless, before 1990, fledgling members of the armed forces could anticipate reliable employment until age 40–50. Demonstrated competence would be necessary to ensure such a career pattern, but subject to that proviso, the future was comfortingly certain. Although periodic job culling did in fact occur prior to 1990, in general such purges did not undermine a prevailing belief that working for the military constituted as reliable a form of employment as could be attained anywhere.

That military employment *was* more certain and dependable than anything prevailing in the civilian world was seen as only just by Service members. After all, it was *they* who were potentially risking life and limb, suffering exposure to geographical turbulence and the disruptions of marital separation on behalf of their compatriots. At the very least, in equity such a contract demanded that military employment remained secure. However, the cessation of the Cold War and the resulting personnel reductions have destroyed this presumption. Both for British and American military members, unemployment emerged as a serious threat to job expectations. Suddenly, at the behest of Treasury demands, the Services were to be exposed to the undiluted play of market forces. Moreover, at least for UK Service personnel, such a process was to be set against a background of chronic recession severely prejudicing alternative civilian work prospects.

How will work motivation respond to an end to job security and abrupt exposure instead to the bitter winds of economic change? Will Service personnel seek to limit the inherent risks involved in their occupation if the carrot of dependable employment disappears? In the mid-1970s, Jacques van Doorn of Erasmus University at Rotterdam in the Netherlands predicted major forthcoming changes in military attitudes. Under the heading 'The Decline of the Mass Army in the West' van Doorn speculated:

> The age of the mass army is past. The current diplomatic detente between NATO and the Warsaw Pact is but one manifestation of this fact. Of greatest importance is the increasing pressure on the system of mass conscription – the basis of the mass army. With the decline in the legitimacy of the military, a structural change is occurring . . . the intimate link between the national army and the nation is dissolving, and 'The Nation in Arms' is no longer a viable concept.
>
> With the end of the draft, and military cutbacks in many countries, armed forces have become smaller, more technically articulated

and less oriented to social patriotism. Among the possible consequences of this shift are the advent of mercenary armed forces
with little public support, a decline in social representation, a conservative outlook in the military, and the assumption of labour
market orientation, including unionization.

(J van Doorn in *Journal of Armed Forces and Society*,
Winter 1975)

Currently, trade union affiliation is illegal for members of
British and American armed forces. In principle, the duty of all
commanders to give first priority to ensuring the welfare of
their staff should make the protection offered by such external
agencies unnecessary. In practice, such proclaimed high standards have not always been achieved. Even if commanders
demonstrate an unrivalled concern for military personnel
through the traditional ethos of safeguarding their interests,
such a protective remit runs neither in the world beyond the
military, nor in the politico-financial decisions determining
Service careers. If those decisions succeed in destroying the
distinctive ethical and altruistic vocational characteristics exhibited by many members of military communities – by
diminishing the perceived professional status of Service
employment, reducing it instead into a job like any other – it will
scarcely be surprising if people suffering such a serious decline
in their employment conditions engage in countervailing action.

If military employment is perceived by its members as down-
graded in the eyes of the parent society, with the potential
dangers incurred on behalf of the nation no longer meriting
special employment protection, the military may experience
increasing difficulties in recruiting and retaining appropriate
staff. Market forces and the promotion of individualism challenge the logic of subordinating self-interest to the benefit of the
wider community. There is already evidence that re-enlistment
willingness is affected by changes in the values of the employing
institution. Edwin M Wagner examined the re-engagement
intentions of 466 USAF members to investigate whether perceived changes in the nature and values of the Air Force
affected career choices.

What he found was that 'institutional values' – the particular character, tradition and ethos of the organisation – appeared to be more significant than market-based factors such as salaries in influencing re-enlistment. 'Institutional' features were identified as unselfish, appealing to the vocational and charitable personality elements of the airmen, justifying an Air Force career as a 'calling'. In contrast, concentrating on the 'occupational' characteristics of military life compared with other jobs – even where there were undeniable advantages – was less likely to encourage re-engagement (Edwin M Wagner, 'Air Force First-Term Reenlistment: the Effect of Held Values' in *The Journal of Political and Military Sociology*, Winter 1989).

The termination of job security is a symbolic destruction of the particular status which military employees enjoyed in the second half of the twentieth century. Such a development could clearly be expected to damage morale. Measures of morale are regularly obtained in the Services, though isolating one particular contributing factor such as job security is difficult. The British Army's *Officer Continuous Attitude Survey* rates morale under four headings:

- the officers themselves
- their immediate working group
- their unit
- the Army as a whole

Between October 1990 and April 1993 – covering the period in which the British government's Options for Change programme presaged substantial redundancies and the enforced mergers of separate Army units – the indices measuring morale were remarkably constant. There was a slight overall decline in morale, but the range was quite small – the variation between the peak in January 1991 and the nadir in January 1993 was only 9%. For particular rank levels, the state of morale modulated more widely, probably relating to the higher risk of redundancy thought to affect particular ranks. For all officers, irrespective of rank, measured morale was considerably below their degree of 'General Satisfaction with Army Life', which changed very little during this turbulent stage in the Army's history. Not surprisingly, when the degree of satisfaction with job security was assessed, a considerable decline was observed with a 28% fall occurring between January 1991 and January 1992.

In contrast, soldiers expressed a much more bullish approach towards employment security. Their index measuring 'Satisfaction with Job Security' fell by less than 7% throughout the October 1989 to September 1993 period, and it was persistently higher than their general measure of satisfaction with Army life. This might reflect greater confidence amongst soldiers that alternative civilian employment would be easily obtained if the redundancy axe fell, or possibly the knowledge for many younger soldiers that they were not in the age brackets which could be affected by the initial tranches of job cuts. Whatever the reasons, it seems that reduced job security had a more noticeable effect on officers than soldiers. (Army Personnel Research Establishment, *Continuous Attitude Survey (Soldiers)*, (APRE Study PP 3/11) by A Hampson, and *Officer Continuous Attitude Survey* (APRE Study 3/12) by S J E Smith and A Hampson, 1993.)

If it is perceived that there has been some reduction in the moral character and social standing of the armed forces, that their quintessential ethos of solidarity, personal integrity and selfless duty are to be sacrificed to the dictates of the market, can the range of present and predicted military activities offer alternative excitement and a comparable moral challenge to both current Service personnel and future recruits? At first sight, participation in United Nations peacekeeping or relief operations might seem a noble alternative: collaborative internationalism repairing world disorders as opposed to the avaricious nation state pursuing solely its own ends. Making the world a safer place could surely satisfy the highest of idealistic aspirations.

But how far does acting in peacekeeping roles fulfil such visionary ambitions? Is military honour rediscovered in such enterprises? Is the UN worth dying for? Governments committing cadres to multinational forces clearly have their doubts.

Little kudos and no electoral advantage has been identified by American and British politicians in UN operations. In the early 1990s, intervention in Somalia did not raise the status and prestige of American forces, nor did it win votes. Despite strident calls from humanitarian agencies, the British government resisted extensive involvement in Bosnia, citing the dangers of being sucked into an escalating conflict and the military difficulties of disengagement, but acutely conscious too that there was no strong ground swell of public opinion which would deliver political benefits.

From the Service members themselves despatched to undertake peacekeeping roles came reports which mixed professional pride in accomplishing difficult tasks with extreme degrees of personal frustration at their inability to achieve more. Crucially, the roles which circumstances required them to perform left them at the mercy of other actors in the military theatre. With no licence to intervene militarily and enforce a local peace, UN service frequently entailed horrified but impotent observation of the carnage inflicted on local communities, mostly civilian. It also left UN contingents vulnerable to shelling and mortar attacks for which they might only accidentally form the target, but to which they possessed extremely limited rights of retaliation. Critical peacekeeping tasks – such as monitoring cease-fires, identifying and assessing the location and capabilities of rival factions, accompanying the transport of humanitarian aid – do incur substantial physical risk and may call for demonstrations of physical courage which enhance and affirm the honourable nature of military life. The dangers of injury and death were ever present for UN personnel, but the military responses for which they were trained in their national Services and which justified their pride in their professional skills were disallowed as possible solutions. Interposition between warring factions demands particular skills and unlimited patience and does not necessarily fit easily with the prior background and expectations of many members of the military. A gung-ho or macho response was invariably inappropriate. Instead, interminable negotiations with local bandit chiefs had to be endured to ease the passage of aid convoys.

However, Charles Moskos detected some status gains for military personnel working for the UN:

> . . . the primitive living conditions of soldiering in the field, the requirements of troop leadership in operational situations, and the ultimate recourse to arms in the always possible event of withstanding assault are all peacekeeping variants of the heroic model (which) accommodates itself to more traditional aspects of soldierly honor.
>
> (Charles C. Moskos Jr, 'UN Peacekeepers:
> the Constabulary Ethic and Military Professionalism' in
> *The Journal of Armed Forces and Society,* August 1975)

Although written 20 years ago, Moskos' observations remain insightful. He studied a sample of the multinational force operating in Cyprus on behalf of the UN, examining both attitudes towards the practices designed to maintain peace and towards the United Nations itself. Did participation in collaborative international intervention promote a positive approach towards the UN or, indeed, towards ideals of world government? What Moskos found was that individual members serving the UN in Cyprus initially divided almost equally in the stance adopted towards the merits of peacekeeping roles – what Moskos termed *the constabulary ethic.* By the sixth month of engagement, however, the proportion reporting positively on the value of low-key peacekeeping activities had almost doubled.

In contrast, the percentage of Service personnel identifying with internationalism moved in the opposite direction: the longer people served, the less internationalist they became. The UN was found wanting in resource provision and decision-making, afflicted with that most serious of civilian diseases: debate followed by inaction. As a result, Moskos was able to see:

> . . . the most dominant characteristic of the military professionalism of the UN peacekeeping soldiers was their maintenance of primary allegiance to their home nationality. It would be very premature to regard military professionalism in peacekeeping forces as a modern

form of the non-national armies of pre-modern Europe. For in addition to the nationalist attitudes uncovered in the interview data, there was also a noticeable propensity among the national contingents of UNFICYP to re-affirm national military traditions through repeated and extended forms of parades, ceremonies and ritualism.

Even peacekeeping service, moreover, was typically interpreted as serving national military purposes: the opportunity for deployment in an overseas environment, the acquisition of experience in multinational military cooperation, and a rationale for an armed forces establishment to counter anti-military domestic opinion. (Moskos, *ibid.*)

Thus, gains may accrue to military institutions from participating in peacekeeping roles, but they appear to be predominantly of a practical, low-intensity nature. Although working for the UN may present opportunities for the honourable discharge of the military ethic, membership of a peacekeeping force does not appear to fulfil optimistic supranational ambitions to promote world harmony. The constraints and limitations surrounding UN activities may well frustrate more than they reward. The UN is a highly flawed jewel, and the limited benefits which ensue from working on its behalf seem unlikely to act as an adequate compensation for the subordination of the virtues of military honour and status to the jungle of market forces.

And if there is to be no special employment protection for members of the armed forces in recognition of the particular hazards of their calling, if working in the Services becomes an occupation like any other and loses its vocational echoes, then the formation of staff associations, a determined assault on the requirement to work anti-social hours and eventually trade union membership must be expected. The nine-to-five soldier, living in private accommodation, working a five-day week and adamant about employment rights gets nearer. Anathema to those still seeking to retain the enshrined military values of total personal commitment, such value changes reflect the subordination of communal concerns to individual gain.

Membership of the armed forces has enjoyed distinct features and values since the Second World War which have marked it out as different in nature from other types of employment. Permitting market forces to reduce it to the status of other occupations and denying its unique nature demeans those traditions and ideals of service to society. Instead, working for the military becomes just like any other occupation, where mercenary considerations become paramount. Perhaps a supply of mercenaries is what British and American governments want: men and women who respond solely to the dictates of economics. But what expectations can be held about the loyalties of military employees if patriotism or internationalism are no longer validated through employment security? Will the calculations of individual financial advantage afford a satisfactory base for ensuring the territorial integrity and national interests of entire communities? Societies get the armed forces they deserve.

Summary
Change has occurred so rapidly for military institutions in the final years of the twentieth century that fundamental modifications in operational practices have become inevitable. Returning USA and British personnel to their home countries to recoup a peace dividend has little-recognised cost implications, particularly in terms of housing, since the housing requirements of returning families have to be repatriated with them. In Britain, new housing arrangements for Service families are likely to terminate a system of universal housing subsidisation. In the longer term, this is likely to produce substantial rent rises and to provide an additional impetus towards owner-occupation, a practice which is obviously facilitated anyway by permanent location in the homeland.

Stationing the armed forces at home will not necessarily reduce marital separation rates – indeed, they may well increase. The obligation to retain the highest degree of technical competence dictates a continuing process of training and exercises, which normally involves separation. That obligation is not going to diminish. There is in addition a pattern of unaccompanied postings where families cannot be safely or practically managed, and the range of such postings is likely to be increased because of the undoubted economic advantages accruing to governments if the need to provide a substantial infrastructure of educational, medical and social supports for accompanying families can be avoided.

Equal opportunities concerns will remain a dominant force for change within the military. Gender and ethnic balances will alter, especially in Britain where issues of ethnic discrimination have only begun to be acknowledged relatively recently.

The exposure of Service personnel to stressful employment – whether arising from overstretch or through harrowing incidents – is potentially an area of considerable financial risk to military employers. Whilst trauma may be seen as a natural operational hazard of Service life, there is now abundant evidence that untreated exposure is damaging to the individuals concerned and operationally debilitating. The threat of legal action, if nothing else, dictates that the armed forces establish pro-active post-trauma services able to provide prompt diagnosis and help.

Finally, the removal of job security for military employees has potentially profound consequences on morale and motivation. Engaging in a dangerous occupation has less obvious attractions if it is no longer compensated for by employment certainty. The disappearance of military job security is symbolic of the declining recognition paid in civilian societies to traditional concepts of military virtue and honour. Working for the United Nations as part of a peacekeeping force, although in principle affording an opportunity for idealism in achieving international collaboration, seems unlikely in practice to be experienced as an uplifting expression of effective international transformation, nor to act as a wholly satisfactory substitute for the loss of a defining military vocation. In 1995, the British government received a report headed by a senior industrialist, Mr Michael Bett, entitled *Review of the Service Career and Manpower Structures and Terms and Conditions of Service of the British Armed Forces.* At the time of writing, the Ministry of Defence's intentions relating to this report are unknown.

Widely publicised have been proposals to slim the rank structure and reduce the number of senior officers. Is this study perhaps the springboard to smaller, highly professional armed forces, affording their members opportunities for a vocational ethos and engendering communal respect?

CHAPTER 9

The Metamorphosis of Military Communities: The Challenge of New Social Structures

The 1970s and 1980s were periods of great *structural* change in the economic, political and cultural foundations of Western society. The changes are long term and set to continue . . Of major importance among them are: the shift from industrialism to post-industrialism and from the national level to the global level in the contemporary capitalist economy; the developments in international political institutions; and the emergence of ecological problems of awesome and unprecedented scale and complexity.
(Maurice Roche, *Rethinking Citizenship*; Cambridge: Polity Press, 1992)

These changes have an immediate impact on the working practices of armed forces – some directly in the form of requirements to adhere to good environmental practices when engaging in training exercises; or in responding to the demands of international bodies. Other effects are more indirect and less visible, but of enormous significance. Like all other areas of public expenditure, military institutions are prey to the dominant crusade mounted by those powerful ideological and financial forces currently orchestrating government activity in post-industrial societies. 'Rolling back the frontiers of the state' or producing

174

'small government' are political objectives with consequences just as serious and contentious for the existence, size and activities of the Services as for publicly funded education or welfare provision.

If the operational world of the military is currently undergoing major transformations in response to the vigour of these ideological and economic forces, the same is also true of the social composition of military communities. The pronounced shift towards becoming predominantly married societies has obliged military authorities to install a range of support systems not required for bachelor Services. Gradually, and not always with enthusiasm, military institutions have come to terms with this new population, sanctioning the provision of education, medical, social welfare and related services essential within young communities where, indeed, in some locations the number of spouses and children comfortably outnumber military employees. Although the majority of Service personnel will start their military career as unmarried, most will marry and parent children during the currency of their military engagement. Many will divorce and remarry. As with civilian communities, a multiplicity of household structures – first marriages, divorcees, divorced single parents, reconstituted second relationships – has become the norm in military societies too. Constant adaptation and fine-tuning of family support structures is required if such support is to remain relevant and an aid to staff retention. The kaleidoscopic nature of contemporary personal relationships compels a continuing reappraisal of their utility by those social support agencies established within the Services to facilitate the combination of a military career with marital and parental ambitions.

Among the important issues needing constant examination are:

- an acceleration of the trend towards the dispersal of military families within civilian communities – increasingly, as far as the UK is concerned – into personal house ownership;
- in consequence there is a concentration of young married couples and young families in Service housing;

- withdrawal from overseas postings will not necessarily reduce separation or tensions within military marriages. Indeed, the experience of the British Royal Navy suggests that marital discord and divorce may rise in such circumstances. Is this a matter which need concern military authorities?
- family support and employee assistance programmes will need careful design, ensuring the availability of advisory and helping systems dealing appropriately, in confidence, with the problems flowing from the management of successive life-stages, recognising the civilian rights and needs of family members not employed by the military, and empowering them to contain and overcome the pressures of Service life;
- improving and extending assistance for military personnel and their families who are making the major transition back into civilian life.

The support offered to Service communities must acknowledge that there are conflicting views within those societies about gender roles and the social conventions of military life. On the one side, the legitimacy of the feminist critique which seeks to advance the status, roles and independence of women both as military employees and as spouses must be acknowledged and the underlying concerns addressed. Paternalistic benevolence, the traditional method both of family support and social control, is condemned as archaic and offensive by such groups.

However, such opinions are not universally held by women in military communities. Some consider that the focus of their loyalties and energies should remain that of successfully adopting the role of the corporate wife, supporting husbands in the pursuit of their careers, which are perceived as primary to the household, and providing assistance to other members of the military community through voluntary endeavours. The study conducted by the US Air Force in 1987 on *Spouse Issues* bears clear witness to this divergence of attitudes. On the one hand, concern was vehemently expressed that dual careers were threatened by military employment and that it was high time the Air Force stopped expecting spouses to provide unpaid community support roles. But there were also powerful voices supporting the continuation of such 'traditional' spouse roles, and general disbelief that spouse activities would in practice be disregarded when candidates were compared for promotion, whatever the declared official USAF policy. Support systems for military communities will thus have to be acceptable to widely diverse groups, offering options of both empowerment *and* assistance, enabling those who wish for employment and social activities independent of the armed forces to achieve those goals, but at the same time legitimising and valuing freely chosen decisions to adopt and sustain roles within Service communities.

MOVING OUTSIDE THE WIRE:
THE DISPERSAL OF MILITARY FAMILIES

Perimeter fencing provides limited access to all military bases. Much military housing is situated within such areas, and families routinely talk of being housed 'inside the wire'. In some locations, being housed in this way has been welcomed as comforting and reassuring, denying easy entry to terrorists or itinerant salesmen. But such security brings with it the disadvantages of isolation from retail, social, educational, sporting and cultural facilities. In the UK, the requirement to make more married quarters available on a large scale from the 1960s onwards as the proportion of married personnel grew meant that much of the newly built housing was necessarily outside the wire. Entire estates of homes were constructed in civilian territory – this was particularly the model adopted for overseas accompanied postings – or in some cases, individual dwellings were purchased or rented by the military authorities and then let to entitled personnel. As far as possible, such external housing provision would nevertheless be geographically nearby so that people living beyond the wire could still partake easily of base facilities. However this was not always possible, either because no suitable housing could be acquired in the immediate locality, or because the positioning of the military base in isolated rural areas meant that there simply *was* no adjacent urban area.

Thus, whilst 'living in married quarters' normally involves accommodation relatively close to the parenting military operation, married quarter estates and singleton dwellings actually came to be dispersed over increasingly wide areas. The expansion of car ownership allowed accommodation to become progressively more distant from the place of employment, and enabled more families to opt for house purchase, although only in the British Royal Navy has house purchase achieved levels comparable with the civilian population. As has been discussed earlier, this reflects in part the Navy's desire to encourage individuals to meet the full costs of housing, but, more fundamentally, it has occurred because of the post-1970 withdrawal of the Navy from world-wide locations. Its subsequent concentration in three base-port areas enabled employees to buy housing in those districts. In contrast, continuing overseas deployments and the employer's expectation that personnel will normally be accompanied by their families wherever they are located has led to house ownership rates which are very much lower in the British Army and RAF.

In 1993, 37.5% of Army families owned houses. (*Wives Continuous Attitude Survey*, p. 47, *op. cit.*), which is in marked contrast to prevailing civilian housing patterns in the last quarter of the twentieth century. Owner-occupation has become the dominant form of British housing tenure, supported by successive governments which have identified both political and economic advantages in privatising housing costs.

United Kingdom Housing Patterns 1947–93

	1947	1981	1993
Owning/ Buying Dwelling	26%	61%	66%
Renting from Public Body	13%	34%	20%
Renting from private landlord or Housing Association	61%	20%	14%

In less than 50 years, Britain moved from being a nation largely of tenants to one of owners. Various forms of tax concessions speeded this process, which in any case clearly reflected popular demand. Ownership was perceived as providing greater family security and stability than a tenancy, and as ownership rates increased, the quality and availability of rented accommodation diminished, so promoting the move into ownership even more firmly. Moreover, the 1993 tenure figures describe the national UK position. Those sections of the population of employment age, however, demonstrate a higher rate of house ownership. So in a society in which civilians in employment have become predominantly purchasers of properties, the prevailing rental patterns characterising military households is even more aberrant.

The regrouping of the Army and the RAF in the UK will in all probability lead to the extension of home ownership among military families so that they come to resemble both the civilian and Naval pattern. The only issue of uncertainty here is the speed with which this change will occur. The collapse in housing prices in Britain since 1988, and, with it, the disappearance of the comforting certainty that property investment guaranteed the acquisition of an inflation-proof asset, may slow down this development, but is unlikely to halt it. Service families will enjoy greater scope to become owner-occupiers, and will undoubtedly exploit this opportunity. By the end of the century, enforced personnel reductions will be complete. The military will remain a major employer, and job prospects – albeit perhaps shorn of significant vocational elements – will be promising for individuals falling within the appropriate age brackets. The enormous financial apparatus constructed to fund house purchase in Britain needs the drive into owner-occupation to continue, and will look very favourably on groups of employees who appear to enjoy reasonably certain employment prospects over the time-frame of a typical mortgage. Service families will be courted by lending agencies anxious for their custom and aware that ownership rates are low amongst such households.

What this will produce are two very disparate communities. On the one hand, substantial numbers of couples will at least start their married and family life in military housing – the easy availability of such housing, even if the rent charges do rise, will remain a prime attraction. But as these families get older, acquire more children, and seek to put down roots in the form of spouse employment and school continuity, the attractions of owner-occupation will become ever more irresistible. Such households will move out of married quarters to establish themselves in their own homes. As a result, they will become dispersed – a military diaspora spread potentially throughout the UK, but, in practice, into areas where some concentration of military employees already exists.

In contrast, the community remaining within married quarters will remain comparatively youthful, negotiating the early stages of marriage and parenting. Youthful inexperience has always been a distinctive feature of military estates, but hitherto there has been a leavening of older families amongst them who have had longer to develop pertinent coping skills and were able to offer both practical support and serve as role models. Military institutions will thus have to develop community and social support systems which can deliver appropriate nurturing care and assistance to the youthful households making up married quarters estates, thus enabling those individuals to acquire their own successful coping strategies for managing the tensions of Service life. At the same time, outreach systems will have to be inaugurated which will permit contact still to be retained with geographically dispersed, house-owning Service families. What type of social support systems appear relevant to these two very different types of military society?

DEVELOPING THE MARRIED QUARTERS COMMUNITY

Future married quarters communities will be even more unbalanced in terms of age structure than in the past. Significant physical distances will separate most of the occupants of military housing from their own extended families and possible kin support. Military authorities could, of course, abandon any commitment to providing systems of support to such communities, depending instead on the intervention of civilian social welfare agencies when emergencies occurred. Such a policy is unlikely to be cost-effective. Civilian agencies become involved with military families only when a crisis has arisen. In the UK, such a crisis normally manifests itself as concern about the abuse, neglect or general safety of a child. In such circumstances, civilian welfare authorities have a statutory duty to become involved. However, this is not the case in sub-crisis situations. On the other hand, marital and parental tensions not sufficiently serious to interest such agencies may nevertheless constitute a crisis for the family concerned. Lack of external support may lead to major anxieties in the household and the loss of operational efficiency on the part of the Service employee.

It is to avoid this outcome that both British and US Services have established in-house welfare support systems, offering help and assistance particularly in those circumstances not judged sufficiently critical to trigger the mediation of statutory authorities. The relocation of the bulk of American and UK personnel in their home territories does not alter the need for such military agencies.

In 1993, the British Treasury suggested that the Ministry of Defence should reduce its expenditure on family and individual welfare on the grounds that such provision was already available from civilian agencies in the UK. To examine this issue, the MoD established a committee of three people to investigate Welfare in the Armed Forces. Chaired by an Army brigadier (Brigadier Adrian Naughten), its other members comprised an RAF Wing Commander with Personnel and Training responsibilities, and an Area Manager in the Naval Personal and Family Service.

This tri-Service committee produced a report which demonstrated that it was difficult, if not impossible, to establish accurate costings for welfare support activities provided within each Service. Specialist in-house agencies, where they existed, could be identified and costed, but the overriding requirement that managers throughout the armed forces accept a responsibility for the welfare of their staff meant inevitably that much interaction between military personnel included a concern about the welfare of individuals, even though the context in which this developed was an interview situation which had been anticipated as being principally concerned with instructional or disciplinary matters.

Explaining the need for welfare, the committee commented: 'Concern with the welfare of Service personnel and their dependants is seen as a legitimate part of human resources management in all three Services. This responsibility forms a crucial part of the management remit placed upon relatively junior managers – for example, Section Commanders, Flight Commanders and Divisional Officers.' The Naughten Report went on to emphasise: 'The recognition of the need for both *reactive/crisis* and *pro-active/preventive* welfare support systems is common to all three Services, though inevitably resource constraints have tended to restrict the development of preventive support.'

Civilian welfare provision was seen as inappropriate and unavailable, in particular because of:

- the unique environment in which Service personnel and their families exist – e.g. military communities;
- the additional stresses and pressures experienced by Service personnel and their families compared to civilians at similar ages and life stages – e.g. separation, familial turbulence etc.; and
- the clear lack of available resources and *understanding* of Service/military procedures within civilian agencies.

The Report of the TriService Welfare Committee went on to describe the demands imposed by change and uncertainty on military life, and concluded not only that concern for the welfare of all personnel remained a legitimate and core feature of the roles performed by all military managers, but that in addition the particular constraints of Service life demanded the continuation of in-house welfare agencies too. No civilian organisations were available to supply pro-active support, but without such support much family and individual distress would occur and retention rates would fall. The committee was required to produce its report in a remarkably short time. As a result, it met only during a three-month period and was obliged to focus specifically on cost questions. Given this hurried timescale, it is not surprising that there were no comparative studies of similar support systems in the US or other NATO armed forces. Nor was the case for a single, unified in-house welfare agency examined in depth. Instead, the Report culminated in a justification of the continuation of single-Service welfare agencies, and a firm assertion that they represented effective resource use. '. . . it is important that the armed forces examine the legitimate (or otherwise) use of the monies they receive. Taking into account the special need that the Services have for comprehensive welfare provision, together with the variety and dedicated effort which exists to meet this need, welfare provision, as it exists today, does represent good value for money.'

This study of Welfare in the Armed Forces was a defensive response from the MoD to Treasury pressure. Whilst it recognised the enormous changes and difficult transition processes currently afflicting military communities, it did not look closely at the increasingly divergent natures of those military communities. Had it done so, it would doubtless have acknowledged the need for very different types of support systems.

EMPOWERING FAMILIES IN MILITARY HOUSING

The exodus of older families from Services housing lowers the age range of those remaining and concentrates in married quarters households particularly vulnerable to the conflicts produced by the interaction of military and personal life. These households will be constructing their marriages, building families and simultaneously learning about the military environment. Unsupported by extended families, the needs of these couples will frequently exceed their own, as yet limited, coping resources. Military institutions must, therefore, identify legitimate areas of intervention and develop helping agencies able to sustain and empower individuals living in married quarters. Critically, assistance must be consciously pro-active – seeking out individuals and groups especially susceptible to marital or parental pressures and bringing forward community integration and support programmes designed to prevent crises occurring.

Such an approach fits well with contemporary interest in the regeneration of communalism in industrial societies. Amorphous urban areas, particularly those which have grown rapidly, fail to create a sense of loyalty or belonging amongst their inhabitants. Instead, isolation, loneliness and feelings of exclusion may typify their reactions. To overcome these sentiments, community development programmes were given high priority. In Britain, such concerns have now returned to fashion after a period of decline since the late 1960s. *Social auditing* or *village appraisal* have become recognised as valuable tools enabling integrative and supportive decisions to be made by both voluntary and publicly funded organisations anxious to deliver their services both relevantly and pro-actively. As a result, models of good community practice developed which can be analysed and adapted to the specific needs of married quarter occupants.

The process begins with a *community profile* which has been defined as: 'A comprehensive description of the needs of a population that is defined, or defines itself, as a community; and of the resources that exist within that community [which allow for] the development of an action plan or other means of improving the quality of life of that community'. (*Community Profiling: Auditing Social Needs*, Murray Hawtin *et al.*; Milton Keynes: Open University Press, 1994). For military institutions, this requires:

- comprehensive information about household sizes, ages, genders; and
- a correlation of these data with information about current deployments so that separated households can be identified.

This will permit the *risk rating* of specific households in terms of probable social, emotional and practical difficulties and therefore create the capacity to target those households for pro-active support. Individuals in such households need sensitive understanding and affirmative action in encouraging and enabling them to engage in social, educational, sporting or other interactive occasions. Such affirmative action may, for example, require preferential entitlement to the use of community resources such as pre-school facilities.

At any one time, different sections or individuals within the married quarters community will be exposed to separation and other major stresses. The pro-active community programme has, therefore, to switch the focus of its activities from time to time. However, in addition to concentrating on current high risk groups, there are two general objectives which effective community programmes must seek to deliver to all residents.

The first is to guarantee that all new arrivals receive a welcoming orientation package designed to ensure not only rapid adjustment to the new physical location but a positive induction into the social systems of the community. Extending further than the provision of written information packs about the new estate, such as the location of medical, shopping and other facilities – practices which military authorities already engage in consistently -- a community integration programme for new arrivals must offer physical escort to social activities, personal introductions to neighbours and achieve the rapid melding of newcomers into their new community. Speedy integration and the swift inculcation of a sense of belonging are critical twin goals for military community development agencies.

The second objective is to provide a continuous, informal educational programme promoting the successful management of marital and family pressures. Married quarters communities need to become learning communities in which there is a mutual transmission of those life-skills which enable individuals to cope productively with family difficulties. Community agency staff must use opportunities to work with individuals so as to help in the development of appropriate responses, but must also provide collective occasions for discussing the best practice in managing separation. Alerting families to the inevitable difficulties provoked by separation, and demonstrating effective management practices is a key task for community staff, and will substantially repay military authorities their resource investment.

Sustaining these young, inexperienced communities demands agency staff with specific abilities. Above all, there has to be an empathy with the circumstances and pressures of the families themselves. Too often in the past, military institutions have employed as local community and estate managers long-Service, or ex-Service, staff with little sympathy for, or understanding of, contemporary young families. The capacity to relate to such people will be essential in the future. Community agencies will need to embrace too contemporary doctrines of client, or consumer, sovereignty, and positively advance democratic practice and control. Residents should not only have the opportunity to take meaningful decisions through representative residents associations about their communities, but receive Residents Contracts which specify not only their housing entitlements and the maintenance obligations of the Defence Housing Executive, but which also outline what is to be expected of community development staff too.

Married quarters communities need customer charters. The organisations delivering housing and community services must create performance indicators allowing residents to measure the level of provision against declared standards. The embryonic Army Families Support Service, intended to provide ongoing welfare support for the British Army as the successor organisation to the Families Housing and Welfare Service from April 1996 is currently constructing just such a customer charter.

Such a cultural shift presents a major challenge. Past practice has frequently depicted married quarters occupants – especially the younger elements – as feckless, irresponsible and inadequate, and, at the same time, highly privileged compared with the hardships endured by preceding generations. Effective community support therefore necessitates the institutional incorporation of an entirely different set of value judgments. Job specifications will emphasise appropriate personal attributes and demonstrated competence in community activism. A lengthy military career is not a sufficient guarantee of essential traits, and may not even be a necessary prerequisite. Ultimately, the goal is to create a community of individuals empowered to solve their own problems, significantly reducing the proportion of difficulties which explode into crises as a result.

THE DISPERSED COMMUNITY:
AN END TO COMPULSORY CONVIVIALITY

The expansion into owner-occupation and away from military housing occurs primarily amongst older and more senior Service families. Apart from significantly altering the age balance of households staying behind in married quarters and removing more worldly wisdom, the exodus into house ownership has important implications for the management of military institutions as well.

In the first place, the withdrawal of older families means that spouses not employed by the military are likely to be living at greater distances from the epicentre of local military organisations. In consequence, their ability to become and remain involved in supportive community roles is much reduced. In Chapter 6 the commitment of spouses to pro-active welfare roles within military bases was shown to be under increasing strain. In part this arose from the rising number of spouses in paid employment and unable to offer time to community activities. But such activities were also perceived as exploitation by spouses who resented being obliged to participate in 'compulsory altruism'. Anxiety that overt resistance would damage the military careers of partners kept people reluctantly in line. No attempt to cost the value to military authorities of such unpaid community services has ever been made. But it is clear that the physical removal of substantial numbers of older spouses from the centre of military areas will reduce that support. The functions undertaken, willingly or otherwise, by older spouses will have now to be provided through welfare agencies, or simply abandoned.

However, it is not only in the disappearance of mutual assistance within the community that increasing home ownership will cast its shadow. The capacity of military institutions to dictate the mores and lifestyles of Service personnel outside the hours of duty will be eroded too. Physical proximity in a military cantonment with a high proportion of employees living and working together enabled military institutions to impose patterns of social control which cannot survive the geographic dispersal of senior households. Such social control structures were created to guarantee the defence and maintenance of those value systems and behaviour patterns which conserved and validated existing military organisations. Control depended on a presumed entitlement of military managers to influence the private and social lives of Service societies. As landlord, the military institution could obviously exercise control over the allocation of married quarters. But typically it chose to impose a much stricter tariff of compliance on its occupants than civilian private landlords did in negotiating terms with tenants. Very strict limitations were imposed on do-it-yourself decoration, permission to keep pets and allowing relatives to stay as guests in married quarters, for example. At the conclusion of a period of occupation, the military landlord required the departing licencees to clean the house and its fittings to a standard of its choice. Failure to conform entailed financial penalties.

Military authorities were thus able to control important aspects of the private lives of their employees, to decree, in effect, the conditions under which those lives would be led. But in addition to influencing domestic lifestyles, the situation in which the great majority of families lived in married quarters enabled a system of societal controls to operate as well through the process of *compulsory conviviality*.

Compulsory conviviality demanded the presence of married couples at formal dinner nights, formal dances and similar occasions. The principal purpose of such events was always to reaffirm the shared values, loyalties and unique features of military life. It constituted a process of inclusive reassurance cementing bonds and sentiments of solidarity. Such social occasions are not unique to the military, of course. They are particularly prevalent in diplomatic or expatriate communities, and private companies also sometimes employ them to reward and bind together existing staff. Enforced conviviality within the military is more formal than amongst civilians, rigidly structured with written rules governing required behaviour. The following stipulations for attending a Dinner Night in a Scottish infantry regiment are typical.

Dinner Night Routine

Attendance/Dress This is a formal occasion to which wives are invited. Mess kit is worn by Mess members.
Dinner Call This is played by the Piper. Members should escort their wives and guests to the places allocated. The seating plan

should be checked beforehand. On arrival at the table everyone should stand behind their seats. Once everyone is in position, Grace will be said after which the ladies should be assisted to sit down.
Dinner The meal is now presented. The waiter serves on the right and collects plates on the left of the person being served. Cutlery should be used from the outside of the place setting, inwards.
The Port After the meal is finished, Port is placed on the table. Each man should fill the glass of the lady on his immediate left and then his own, thereafter the decanter is passed (slid) down the table in a clockwise direction. The Port should not be drunk at this time as it will be required after the Piper plays for the Loyal Toast.
The Loyal Toast The Junior Mess Member stands up, gives three raps of the gavel and proclaims 'Ladies and Gentlemen, please be upstanding'. After everyone has risen he says 'I wish to propose a toast to Her Majesty the Queen'; 'The Queen'. This is then repeated by everyone and the toast drunk.
Leaving the Table The Dinner is now over and everyone may leave the table after the Principal Guests have left. No one should leave the table during the course of the dinner, the obvious exceptions being ladies with *genuine medical problems.* (emphasis added.)

In practice there is some leeway in the application of these rules. Thus, ladies wishing to leave the table are not actually required to submit to medical inspection for official authorisation, and males who collapse on or under the table – whether through imbibing too copiously of the port or for other reasons – are not left lying where they fall. Nevertheless, the existence of dinners such as these enables the military hierarchy to impose its will on the Service community, for there are strong elements of compulsion about such occasions. Failure to attend – for spouses as well as military employees – is regarded seriously. Non-participation in social activities may be interpreted as evidence of non-conformity, and therefore suspect. At the very least, non-attendance excludes the absentee from the rituals of reaffirmed solidarity, and therefore to some extent attaches the label 'outsider' to non-participants.

Compulsory conviviality also enables senior management to supplement their more formal processes of staff evaluation.

The willingness or otherwise of the employee and spouse to interact with others can be observed. The quality of what is said can be assessed. And the degree of enthusiasm with which couples participate can be regarded as an unofficial measure of conformity to organisational values. Information about employees can also be acquired by the chain of command, and this is true not only during formal military dinners, but also on similar occasions arranged by private companies: 'It is amazing how much I have learned about the unknown aspects of my subordinates' personalities through their wives' careless remarks.' (Senior manager commenting in 'Shell Wives in Limbo' by Soraya Tremayne in *The Incorporated Wife* by H Callan and S Ardener (eds); Croom Helm, 1984)

Participation in obligatory dinners, dances and so on does, therefore, present elements of threat. Absence, or refusal to attend, can have damaging career consequences and is not an available coping strategy. These are, literally, occasions not to be missed. Compulsory conviviality thus enables military authorities to require overt demonstrations of compliance with the norms and values prescribed by the organisation to assure its continuation. For those obliged to attend, there are considerable financial consequences. Apart from travel and childminding costs, the clothes demanded for these events demand substantial investment. Military employees are required to buy distinctive uniforms of no utility beyond special Mess functions. Because each Mess wishes to affirm its own unique history and identity, such attire is manufactured in extremely limited quantities, and therefore prices are high. Wives accompanying military husbands complain of the costs of acquiring formal evening wear, and updating or changing it regularly.

This process of social control is clearly much more difficult to enforce once constituent families become dispersed into the wider civilian society. The strong desire felt by some couples to escape the pressures to participate in enforced conviviality provides an extra incentive to abandon life in married quarters and move away from the military base area. There are, then, a number of social and familial factors which further the drive towards house ownership in addition to those economic pressures which are particularly marked in Britain. Is the diaspora of Service households scattered within civilian areas to be regarded as a community in any meaningful sense? If it is, in what ways can its identity be confirmed and its singular concerns addressed?

REACHING OUT: STRENGTHENING
TENUOUS LINKS BEYOND THE WIRE

'Community' is an elusive concept. It has been widely used to imply something in common to a group or section of the population, and has often been seen as grounded in geographical propinquity. Since 1961 in Britain, 'community' has also been attached to a number of government initiatives – such as community care; community development; and Community Charge – which have aroused varying degrees of support or antagonism. In consequence, 'community' itself has sometimes been tarnished as an idea because of what it has been associated with.

Physical location is not, however, necessarily the only or even principal defining characteristic of a 'community'. Certainly in both Britain and the United States, it is meaningful to talk of a 'Jewish community', the 'Catholic community', or of a community based on ethnic origin. What these examples of community have in common is a 'community of interest', and it is in this sense that Service families, wherever they are physically located, continue to comprise an identifiable community. It is abundantly clear that such families are exposed to circumstantial pressures which are largely unique to them, and which are certainly not experienced to the same degree of intensity by most civilians. Many of those pressures will continue to exist – notably separation – even if house purchase does enable others such as spouse employment and educational continuity for children to be managed more easily. It would be unwise and counter-productive for military authorities to take the view that people who have chosen to move away from married quarters no longer deserve support. But even if that viewpoint is accepted, there are obvious practical problems in maintaining contact with dispersed Service families. Two possible ways forward are examined here:

1. The feasibility of deploying Service welfare agency personnel to visit such households.
2. The provision of outreach resources to those self-help systems already in place within military societies which would enable them to maintain contact.

Deploying Service Welfare Personnel

It is not possible to see such staff engaged pro-actively in visiting dispersed families. The numbers are too small, and there are more urgent demands on their professional skills in the married quarters communities now denuded of older residents. In practice, visits by welfare staff to dispersed families are only likely to occur when a crisis situation has arisen for the family, the solution to which affects the deployment of a Service employee. Manning decisions to relocate personnel in order to help them manage overwhelming marital or family problems will continue to be preceded by social enquiry reports from the Service welfare agency. Such reports can only be compiled after a domestic visit to the household. Thus, Service welfare staff will continue to maintain contact with families when it is necessary to assist them in reacting to a crisis, but that is effectively the limit of such involvement.

A subsidiary degree of professional support to families could be constructed through the Services welfare agencies contracting with the extensive SSAFA network throughout the UK. This comprises (genuine) volunteers who deliver a low-key system of information gathering for Service personnel concerned about members of their extended families. A young man who knows that domestic violence has featured in his parents' marriage and is worried that he has received no recent contact from his mother can ask a SSAFA volunteer to call and check her well-being. This valuable process could be extended with appropriately trained volunteers – possibly receiving some payment in recognition of their specialised role – routinely visiting all dispersed Service families subject to separation. The visitors need to be sufficiently skilled to recognise how competently or otherwise the household is managing the absence of the Service employee; to offer friendship and company to the spouse; and to alert the Service welfare agency where major difficulties were clearly developing.

This would make demands on military resources, but could enhance the symbiotic relationship which currently exists between SSAFA and UK military authorities. The SSAFA local network of volunteers extends throughout the United Kingdom and Eire. It is an unrivalled instrument for reaching out to distant families. Yet its *raison d'être* has lain largely in providing information reports about kin to Service personnel, many of whom could not make personal contact with their families because of overseas postings. Repatriation implies that this particular demand on the SSAFA network will decline. Alternative roles will therefore be needed to avoid atrophy. Acting in a direct agency capacity for Service welfare bodies could obviously be one such role.

The second positive approach to reaching out to dispersed families is for the chain of command to delegate much of this function to military self-help agencies. The development of the Federation of Army Wives was briefly described in Chapter 6. With its companion body The Association of RAF Wives, much has been achieved in promoting the concerns of families within military communities. Housing, education and disability rights have all featured significantly in the campaigns orchestrated by such Associations. Annual Conferences have provided a productive forum to unleash informed, trenchant attacks directed at government Ministers presiding over enforced redundancy programmes. Most valuably, these Associations have produced quarterly journals focusing on the concerns of wives and families generally. These publications are, in effect, subsidised by military institutions through free delivery using military personnel.

Families living at a distance from the base clearly cannot have this invaluable information source freely delivered. But it would be a sensible investment for Service authorities to agree to meet postage costs. Journals addressing the particular concerns of military families provide a formidable tool for reinforcing common bonds and loyalties. Specifically local information, applicable to each military unit alone, could be added to the journals in the form of loose-leaf insertions by that unit before postage. In this way, military authorities would succeed in maintaining linkages between Service families, however geographically distant they might be, though only on the terms agreeable to the self-help bodies whose outreach capacities they would be utilising.

In these various ways, both a pro-active and reactive support system could continue to extend to Service households wherever they lived. Increased home ownership does not remove the myriad pressures to which military life subjects its families. The justification for maintaining employee assistance or support programmes is in the beneficial pay-off to the employer. Effective outreach approaches will continue to deliver such benefits to military authorities.

MOVING ON

For many Service families, leaving a military engagement and acquiring civilian status is the ultimate anxiety. Whatever the disadvantages of living in high visibility in the 'goldfish bowl' atmosphere of a married quarters community, there is nevertheless comforting familiarity and shared solidarity. Such assurances inevitably are removed when military employment contracts are terminated. The civilian world may seem strange, unattractive and threatening, and it is abundantly clear that the transition into it represents a frightening experience for many Service personnel. Both in Britain and America, specialist agencies within the armed forces seek to prepare individuals for discharge. The support facilities provided have considerably improved as a result of the early 1990s redundancy programme. Nevertheless, there are substantial differences in practice as to the degree of assistance provided. A notable feature of American resettlement programmes is the inclusion of family dependants. In contrast, the British armed forces have proved very reluctant to extend resettlement packages to spouses, and not at all to other family dependants.

Under the impetus of the Options for Change programme, the Ministry of Defence established the Tri-Service Resettlement

Organisation (TSRO) in 1990. This brought together many of the existing single-Service resettlement resources, but amplified the prestige attached to the process by heading up the new agency with a Major General. Its official remit comprised: '(being) broadly responsible for organising the collective features of MoD's resettlement provision. This includes briefings, training courses, the principal resettlement publications and the services provided by the Services Employment Network.' However, in addition, military employees can also seek advice from their own employing Service since: 'The single Services are . . . responsible for the provision of a resettlement advisory service which is available to individuals throughout their Service careers' (Tri-Services Resettlement Organisation, *Resettlement Handbook*; 1993).

The TSRO offers a range of helpful services. These include:

- job-search briefings;
- career briefings;
- an extensive range of in-house resettlement training courses; and
- MoD sponsored courses delivered by other agencies.

Eligibility for TSRO facilities is largely determined by length of Service. Personnel with less than five years' Service are normally excluded, though they may be able to participate in certain training courses on a fill-up basis if there are course vacancies. To date, the MoD has not granted resettlement training to spouses, despite pressure from the Federation of Army Wives, apparently on the grounds that offering resettlement services to dependants would be seen as poaching, and so unacceptable competition, by other education agencies also receiving public funding. In any case, such discussions as have occurred around this issue have only been based on the possibility of spouses participating on a make-weight basis, comparable to short-service personnel also otherwise excluded from the system. The MoD has never acknowledged that spouses and other family dependants constitute a group towards which they have any resettlement responsibilities *per se*. Insofar as dependants are being recognised at all in this context, it is purely as regrettable accretions of the employed individual to whom the system has undeniable responsibilities.

This mean-minded approach is in marked contrast to US practice. The Family Support Center of the US Air Force, for example, is tasked with delivering a Transition Assistance Program (TAP), which provides separating or retiring members *and their families* with the skills and knowledge required to make a successful transition to a second career or retirement. Program Objectives include:

*   transition counselling;
*   pro-active career planning;
*   development of job search skills; and
*   increased access to employment opportunities and information.

For retiring family members a Transition Manager is required to provide a relevant transition programme. This can comprise both directly provided support services – including employment-oriented education – or the purchase of skills from external consultants. Within this system, spouses have equal rights of entitlement. The process thus recognises that the resettlement of a married military employee entails the resettlement of a family, and acknowledges the rights of other family members to have their transition needs attended to. Such an approach makes much sense, since a resettlement system which ignores, or fails to build up, spouse skills and employment opportunities cannot constitute best possible practice in the advice and assistance given to the employee. Where the family should be advised to direct its interests in the civilian world must be affected by the talents and abilities possessed by *all* family members. Neglecting some of them can only be counterproductive.

That the British Defence Ministry has advanced less down this path than the USAF is no doubt partly an issue of expense, since providing resettlement facilities to dependants as a matter of right would cost more. But it is also symbolic of the slow progress being made within the British armed forces towards the recognition of spouses and other family members as people existing in their own right.

Summary

This Chapter has examined the creation of two very different kinds of Service communities. On the one hand, the married quarters community of families living in military housing will continue to exist despite the increased number of military employees becoming home owners away from the base. However, married quarters will predominantly contain young couples and young families. It is the older and more life-experienced members of military societies who will move into owner-occupation. This has important consequences for Service welfare agencies. The approach to such youthful married quarters communities will have to be consciously pro-active, recognising the vulnerable nature of such demographically atypical neighbourhoods and identifying groups and individuals at particular risk on whom resources should be concentrated in a bid to prevent crises happening. Welfare, and housing agency, staff will have to empathise with young people in these early life-stages.

Separation rates are unlikely to decline, and may increase if currently accompanied postings fall victim to cost-cutting. Enabling people to manage marital and family separations successfully remains a key welfare task.

This is true also for the second, emerging military community, which consists of private house owners dispersed throughout civilian areas. Reaching out to such households demands a creative use of existing welfare resources, and the delegation of added responsibility, with appropriate official funding, to self-help organisations. Dispersal reduces traditional systems of social control which military managers have been able to impose as a function of geographical proximity. To escape such controls may well act as an incentive for some families to leave married quarters.

Finally, systems designed to assist personnel leaving the armed forces and moving into civilian life need to acknowledge the rights of dependants. That spouses need retraining for the civilian world is at least in part because they *are* military spouses, and have suffered disruptions in their lives well in excess of their civilian counterparts. The provision of resettlement services to them in their own right would therefore seem no more than an equitable compensation.

CHAPTER 10

Conclusions:
Forward March?

The overwhelming impression I gained from the Service spouses I talked to in the course of the study was their feeling that they and the contribution they make in support of the Australian Defence Force are not valued either within the Service community or in the community generally. They perceive the Service hierarchy as generally unsympathetic to the special problems Service life creates for a family, and inflexible in responding to those problems. They see the civilian community generally as placing little value on defence activities and having little or no esteem for those who choose defence as a career or for their families.

(Supporting Service Families: A Report on the Main Problems facing Spouses of Australian Defence Force Personnel and Some Recommended Solutions by Sue Hamilton; Canberra: Office for the Status of Women, 1986)

The difficulties experienced by British and American military families are not unique to those societies alone, as this extract from a recent Australian review of the concerns of Service families there makes clear. All countries which create professional armed forces to sustain their own territorial integrity and to promote supra-national political objectives present similar demands to military employees: an overriding requirement to combine the maintenance of the highest attainable level of military competence with instant operational readiness in any global theatre.

Such a demand interferes profoundly with the construction of a private, personal life. Because it makes economic sense for professional military forces to retain over a substantial number of years people they have invested considerable sums in recruiting and then processing through a continuous and costly training programme, it inevitably follows that an increasing proportion of military employees will marry and parent during their careers. Not only will they marry for the first time, a sizeable fraction will divorce and re-marry. A smaller percentage will consist of single parents who seek to combine Service employment with sole adult oversight of developing children. The demographic structure of military communities has undergone a revolution, towards which the British and American Services in particular have made sometimes reluctant, hesitant and uncertain responses.

Reacting appropriately is above all an issue of *attitudinal change*. Military institutions must acknowledge the dramatic changes which have affected their own populations and the legitimacy of the demands for the right to marry, have children and a private life – areas where the Service must no longer seek to enforce outmoded patterns of social control. In their conclusions to the study on *Army Wives* the authors commented:

> The regimental system of voluntary support in general remains hierarchical and paternalistic. It engenders a feeling of apathy amongst the more intelligent wives of junior ranks who feel they can achieve little for themselves. Officers' wives no longer feel they have the right to become involved in 'social work'; many do not want to either . . .The ideal of trust and communication between all levels in a regiment has been eroded. Instead, there is a 'Fear of the Chain of Command' which prevents problems being raised. There is a corresponding fear by the chain of command which prevents problems being aired outside the regimental system to preserve its good name.
>
> (*The Army Wives Study* by Colonel M and Mrs J Gaffney; Ministry of Defence, 1986)

Military institutions have to come to terms with demographic reality. Not only do a majority of professional Service personnel marry, the resulting pattern of family structures is very varied. However much the armed forces might wish to recognise and sustain only one particular, socially approved family type, there is in practice the same heterogeneous collection of family styles found within Service communities as in the wider society outside. One of the prerequisites for meaningful support structures for families is to accept this diversity, and to respond appropriately to the differing needs demonstrated by different households.

Sue Hamilton made this comment about attitudes towards families by the Australian Defence Department:

> . . . some of the current attitudes I have observed and which have been reported to me are based on a particular view of the role of the family and the relationships of individuals within it – one which assumes that the needs and interests of all other members should be subordinated at all times to those of one breadwinner. This model of the family has been a convenient one for the Services in the past, but, while it remains a legitimate choice for some families, it is by no means the preferred model for many Australian families today, and, unless some means can be found to respond more adequately to the varying needs of families, it seems likely that a defence career will become increasingly incompatible with a satisfactory family life for a growing number of people.
>
> (Hamilton, *Supporting Service Families*; *op. cit.*)

Accepting the entitlement of spouses to work outside the military community is certainly an important part of the necessary changes in attitude. In America, the US Air Force *Spouse Issues* Report reached the firm conclusion:

> The final recommendation is that the Air Force needs to actively support the career and employment aspirations of Air Force spouses. To support these employment aspirations, the Panel recommends the Air Force further develop its spouse employment programs. This task should be accomplished within the Family

Support Centers. Such programs could include assistance in personal skills assessment, job banks, resumé clinics and advanced employment prior to permanent-change-of-station moves. The Air Force must actively promote among civilian business leaders the importance and benefits of hiring military spouses.

(US Air Force Blue Ribbon Panel Report on *Spouse Issues*;
Washington DC: Pentagon, 1986)

Such an activist approach contrasts markedly with that adopted by the British Service authorities. As we have seen, in the UK spouses do not receive any automatic right to resettlement education or training before a military family re-enters civilian life. Nor is a spouse – or other family dependant – seen as a legitimate focus of resettlement provision. Assisting spouses to improve their employment opportunities whilst still within the military system is equally not accepted as a proper use of Service resources. The updating and skills-enhancement programmes which do exist specifically for spouses derive from voluntary self-help agencies like the Federation of Army Wives. For military authorities, this represents a commendable community initiative which incurs very little public expense and helps to prevent the natives becoming restless. Of course, it can be argued that the armed forces cannot be expected to do more to enable spouses to undertake careers of their own than any other employer might do – and civilian employers do not routinely provide employment training for the spouses of their employees. But civilian spouses invariably have access to near-by educational and training facilities which are not available to their military counterparts. Moreover, civilian spouses are not subjected to the same degree of spatial dislocation and required to move with the same frequency as Service families. Such turbulence obviously makes the completion of training courses extremely difficult. By offering either financial support so that individuals could purchase distance learning packages, or by delivering relevant training to spouses direct, military authorities would be no more than compensating their families for the disruptions caused by the exigencies of Service life.

Ultimately what is unavoidable is for Service institutions to accept that spouses and other family members are civilians; have no obligations whatsoever to the armed forces; and must be enabled to enjoy the rights and opportunities open to other civilians in the society beyond the camp gates. The conviction held for so long by military authorities that they *own* their employees and can properly demand their complete time and attention throughout their waking hours is itself unlikely to survive much longer. The extension of such demands to the employee's family through a network of social controls governed by the fear that non-conformity would damage the Service career must be abandoned.

The retention of highly skilled personnel will be much more effectively guaranteed by family support and employee assistance programmes which start from the current pattern of households as they actually exist within Service communities; which devise helping systems relevant to the particular circumstances of different types of household; which can be used in confidence and without threat to military careers; and which, above all, *empower* spouses to take control of their own lives.

Empowerment is in part affected by posting decisions. Fewer moves would clearly allow easier life-planning. The justification for regular postings was to some extent challenged in Britain in the early 1990s by the concept of the 'smaller but more stable' Army. The theory was that repatriation from continental Europe to the United Kingdom should be accomplished so that all units within the Army had defined geographical base areas where they could normally expect to be located. Up to now, the objectives of stability and less frequent redeployment have been negated by the complications of regimental and unit amalgamation induced by the Options for Change programme, and the continuing demands for unaccompanied postings to Northern Ireland and in United Nations operations.

Less frequent moves obviously would allow families to spend more time together, and spouses could seek employment or training opportunities with more certainty that they would be living in the same location long enough to make use of them.

However, empowerment means more than this. It demands that military institutions abandon any claims on the time and energies of spouses. It means developing customer charters in which spouses are identified as important individuals with legitimate needs which the military has no right to deny. It means amending institutional structures so that spouses are acknowledged *and valued* as individual beings in their own right. Above all, it means letting go – withdrawing from the traditional methods of controlling the energies and activities of military community members, from trying to channel those energies and activities into a limited number of 'Service approved' patterns of behaviour. Letting go means *trusting* the community to make decisions for itself, *believing* that individuals are the best judges of their own cause; and *encouraging* a network of sensitive, varied and supportive helping networks, both voluntary and also financed by Defence funds. This would manifest truly the demise of traditional military attitudes.

The armed forces are moving into uncharted territories. But:

One does not discover new lands without consenting to lose sight of the shore for a very long time.

(André Gide, *The Counterfeiters*)

Bibliography

Adorno, T, *The Authoritarian Personality*, New York, 1950.

Army General Administrative Instruction, *Licence to Occupy a Married Quarter*, Issue 101, Annex B/84, Ministry of Defence, 1991.

Ball, M, Harloe, M and Martens, H, *Housing and Social Change in Europe and the USA*, Routledge, 1988.

Boulegue, J, '"Feminization" and the French Military: an Anthropological Approach', in *Journal of Armed Forces and Society*, Vol. 17, Spring 1991.

Brannen, J and Moss, P, (Eds), *Re-Assessing Fatherhood*, Sage, 1987.

Burgoyne, J, Ormrod, R and Richards, M, *Divorce Matters*, Penguin, 1987.

Casey, J, *The History of the Family: New Perspectives on the Past*, Blackwell, 1989.

Clapham, D, Kemp, P and Smith, S, *Housing and Social Policy*, Macmillan, 1990.

Coser, L, *Greedy Institutions: Patterns of Undivided Commitment*, New York, Free Press, 1974.

Cole, I and Furbey, R, *The Eclipse of Council Housing*, Routledge, 1994.

Clulow, C, *To Have and to Hold: Marriage and the First Baby*, University of Aberdeen Press, 1975.

Department of Defense, *Executive Summary: 1992 DoD Surveys of Officers and Enlisted Personnel and their Spouses*, Washington, The Pentagon, 1993.

Breaking Ranks

Doering, Z D and Hutzler, W P, *Description of Officers and Enlisted Personnel in the United States Armed Forces*, Rand, 1982.

Doorn, J van, 'The Decline of the Mass Army', in *Journal of Armed Forces and Society*, Winter 1975.

Dreitzel, H, (Ed.), *Recent Sociology*, Macmillan, New York, 1970.

Dugdale, J, *Developing Reorientation and Educational Guidance Programmes for Redundant Armed Forces Personnel and their Spouses*, University of Bristol Department for Continuing Education (unpublished), 1994.

Enloe, C, *Does Khaki Become You?*, Pandora, 1988.

European Community Directorate of Social Affairs, *A Social Portrait of Europe*, Brussels, 1991.

Finch, Wing Commander R, *RAF Welfare Organization*, Ministry of Defence, 1978.

Freud, S, 'Three Contributions to the Theory of Sex', in *The Standard Edition of the Complete Psychological Works of Sigmund Freud* (Ed. J Strachey), Hogarth Press, London, 1966.

Gaffney, Colonel M and Mrs J, *The Army Wives Study*, Ministry of Defence, 1987.

Gibran, K, *The Prophet*, Heinemann, 1926.

Gibson, C, *Dissolving Wedlock*, Routledge, 1994.

Gross, R, *Psychology: the Science of Mind and Behaviour*, Hodder & Stoughton, 1987.

Hamilton, S, *Supporting Service Families: A Report on the Main Problems Facing Spouses in the Australian Defence Force Personnel and Some Recommended Solutions*, Office for the Status of Women, Canberra, 1986.

Hampson, A and Smith, S J E, (Eds), *Continuous Attitude Surveys: Officers* (Report 93R027); *Soldiers* (Report 93R037); *Wives* (Report 94R023), Army Personnel Research Establishment, Ministry of Defence, 1994.

Harris, S E, 'Military Policies Regarding Homosexual Behaviour: an International Survey', in *Journal of Homosexuality*, Vol. 21, 1991.

Harry, J, 'Homosexual Men and Women who Served their Country', in *Journal of Homosexuality*, Vol. 10, 1984.

Hawtin, M, Hughes, G and Percy-Smith, J, *Community Profiling: Auditing Social Needs*, Open University Press, 1994.

Jolly, *Military Man, Family Man: Crown Property?*, Brassey's, 1987.

Jowell, R and Airey, C, (Eds), *British Social Attitudes Surveys*, Dartmouth Publishing, 1984, 1989.

Bibliography

Klick, J E, 'Utilization of Women in the NATO Alliance', in *Journal of Armed Forces and Society*, Vol. 4, Summer 1978.

Mansfield, P and Collard. J, *The Beginning of the Rest of Your Life: Portrait of Newly Wed Marriage*, Macmillan, 1988.

Ministry of Defence, *Army Welfare Inquiry* (Chairman: J Spencer), 1975.

Ministry of Defence, *Discipline and Standards Paper*, 1993.

Ministry of Defence, *Report of the Naval Welfare Committee*, (Chairman F Seebohm), 1974.

Moskos, C, 'UN Peacekeepers: The Constabulary Ethic and Military Professionalism', in *Journal of Armed Forces and Society*, Vol. 1, 1975.

Moskos, C, 'Female GIs in the Field', in *Journal of Armed Forces and Society*, Vol. 11, Autumn 1985.

Moss, P, *Childcare and Equal Opportunity*, Report of the European Commission, Brussels, 1988.

Naughten, Brigadier A, *TriService Review of Welfare*, Ministry of Defence, 1993.

Oakley, A, *The Sociology of Housework*, Blackwell, 1974.

Owen, W, *The Poems of Wilfred Owen*, Chatto, 1990.

Parkinson, F, *Post-Trauma Stress*, Sheldon Press, 1993.

Parry, G, *Coping with Crises*, Routledge, 1990.

Ramsey, Brigadier G, *Coordination of Welfare Services in BAOR*, Ministry of Defence, 1989.

Roche, M, *Rethinking Citizenship*, Polity Press, 1992.

Robinson, M, *Family Transformation during Divorce and Remarriage*, Routledge, 1991.

Rothberg, J M, 'Stress and Suicide in the US Army: Effects of Relocation on Service Members' Mental Health', in *Journal of Armed Forces and Society*, Vol. 17, Spring, 1991.

Schoenberg, E and Humphries, C P, *Separation Study*, (Annexe to Ministry of Defence *Naval Welfare Committee* Report), 1974.

Schwartz, J B, Wood, L L and Griffith, J D, 'The Impact of Military Life on Spouse Labor Force Outcomes', in *Journal of Armed Forces and Society*, Vol. 17, Spring 1991.

Schutz, A, 'The Concept of Action', in *The Collected Papers of A. Schutz*.

Segal, M W, 'The Military and the Family as Greedy Institutions', in *Journal of Armed Forces and Society*, Vol. 13, Fall 1986.

Shea, N, *The Army Wife*, Harper & Row, 1966.

Stanhope, H, *The Soldiers: an Anatomy of the British Army*, Hamish Hamilton, 1979.

Stiehm, J, 'Managing the Military's Homosexual Exclusion Policy', in *University of Miami Law Review*, Vol. 46, 1992.

Storr, A, *The Integrity of Personality*, Penguin, 1960.

Thornes, B, and Collard, J, *Who Divorces?*, Routledge, 1979.

United States Air Force, *Family Support Center Program*. AF Regulation 30 – 7, 1991. Air Force Instruction 36 – 3009, 1994.

United States Air Force, *Spouse Issues*, Blue Ribbon Panel Report, The Pentagon, 1986.

Wilders, M, *Army Welfare: Survey for the Army Welfare Inquiry Committee*, Ministry of Defence/HMSO, 1977.

Young, M and Willmott, P, *The Symmetrical Family*, Routledge, 1973.

Name Index

Subject Index

Subject Index

SSAFA 191–2
Start Right Royal Society of Arts Report
  9
Stress 157–8
  post-trauma 159–62

Trade unionism and military life 2, 165,
  170
Transition Assistance Program 196
TriService Review of Welfare Report

181–2
TriService Resettlement Organization
  195
United Nations
  peacekeeping role 167
  and military morale 168–70
*United States Armed Forces: Description of
  Officers & Enlisted Personnel* 5

Wives clubs 103, 105, 117